# State College, Pennsylvania

*a Photographic Celebration*

Centennial
State College · Pennsylvania
1 8 9 6 — 1 9 9 6

# STATE COLLEGE, PENNSYLVANIA
## *a Photographic Celebration*

*a publication of the State College Centennial
Commission of the Borough of State College*

*Centennial*
State College · Pennsylvania
1 8 9 6 — 1 9 9 6

For more information, please contact: The State College Centennial Commission of the Borough of State College, 118 South Fraser Street, State College, Pennsylvania 16801. Telephone: 814-234-7110.

Library of Congress Catalog Card Number 95-70705

ISBN  0-9647274-1-2 *(if hardback)*
ISBN  0-9647274-6-3 *(if softback)*

First Printed in October 1995 by
Seneca Printing, Franklin, Pennsylvania

BOOK DESIGNERS: GRETL AND JAMES COLLINS

*This book is dedicated to
all who love State College.*

This book was made possible
through the generous assistance of:

*Centre Daily Times*

*The Corner Room*

*Eastman Kodak Company*

*The Film Center*

*HRB Systems*

*Kissinger, Bigatel, & Brower Realtors*

*Mellon Bank*

*Old Main Frame Shop & Gallery*

*PNC Bank*

*The Rittenhouse Family — McDonald's*

*Sheckler Photographics Custom Lab*

*Uni-Marts*

## One Day in State College, Pennsylvania—September 12, 1994

State College has endeared itself to residents and visitors for 100 years. Incorporated as a borough on August 29, 1896, it still bears architectural evidence of its Victorian origins, when horses, not cars, carried people along College Avenue.

The forces of the twentieth century have transformed State College from a small town adjoining Penn State to an emerging metropolis with an identity and destiny singularly its own. It is not what it was a century ago, and it is not yet what it will become in the next century. That is why, in anticipation of our town's 100 birthday on August 29, 1996, the State College Centennial Commission committed itself to sponsoring a community photography project that would preserve forever the State College we know today.

Altogether, 195 volunteers became the Corps of Centennial Photographers. The mission: to photograph the State College area during the twenty-four hours of one day – an exercise that would cause us to examine ourselves as a community on the cusp of its centennial.

Three tenets guided this project.
1. Photographs are valuable for their artistic, evocative, and descriptive powers.
2. Anyone can make important images.
3. Time bestows upon photographs even greater aesthetic intrigue and historical significance.

The photographers represent a wide range of ages, professions, and photographic approaches. They are kindergarten, elementary, high school and college students, and their teachers. They are photojournalists, commercial photographers, fine arts photographers, photo hobbyists, and people with little or no photographic experience.

They came from State College and other Centre County communities like Lemont and Boalsburg. A few came from other parts of the state and country. All participated from a love of State College, from a sense of adventure, and from a respect for the contribution that photography can make to our local history. Enthusiastic and dedicated to the purpose of producing a permanent record, the photographers donated their own equipment and materials.

The designated shoot day, Monday, September 12, 1994, was chosen for being an ordinary weekday when people would go about their daily routines at home, work, and school. Intrepid photographers began shooting at midnight and continued on through the dark, quiet hours of the early morning.

A blinding sunrise greeted the next wave of photographers. By mid-morning, the sky was a brilliant blue. Clear and crisp, the air crackled with the energy of nearly 200 frenetic photographers scurrying around. Most were working on specific assignments. Others were roving the streets in search of serendipity. Encountering each other throughout the day, the photographers told tales about their adventures, shared tips, and inspired one another.

Certain photographers assigned themselves to cover the surrounding townships. We welcomed this look outward. Although the "Borough of State College" denotes a legally defined governmental zone, the term "State College" connotes a lifestyle that includes visits to special places near, but outside of, the borough borderline, like Meyer Dairy and Mount Nittany.

Evening brought the photographers new challenges. Tired, but still fueled by adrenaline, they scrambled to capture as many subjects as possible within the remaining few hours. By midnight, they had snapped approximately 4,500 pictures, 234 of which are included here.

No community can be documented comprehensively in twenty-four hours. At the outset, we knew that this project, by its very nature, would yield an archive about State College that would be idiosyncratic and incomplete. Nevertheless, what unfolds in this photo essay is telling of this town's hold on its citizens.

Our thanks to all who graciously opened their hearts and gave their financial support for this civic self-portrait. We hope that copies of this book will be discovered in State College attics a century from now. May you of the future enjoy these photographs and thereby remember us as a community that took pride in itself.

— Maryann Curione

— Lurene Frantz

— Steve Williams
   Project Directors

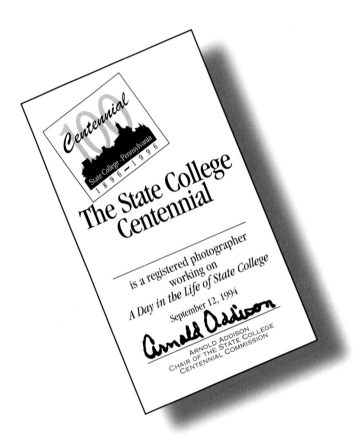

## The State College Centennial

Centennial 100
State College · Pennsylvania
1 8 9 6 — 1 9 9 6

is a registered photographer
working on
*A Day in the Life of State College*

September 12, 1994

*Arnold Addison*

ARNOLD ADDISON
CHAIR OF THE STATE COLLEGE
CENTENNIAL COMMISSION

*Official badge worn by the Centennial project photographers*

*Photographs are like seeds.*

*Time transforms them.*

*Snapshots become emblems.*

*Photographs pierce history's haze and bear today*
*into tomorrow.*

*This book's images will be appreciated most*
*by those not yet born.*

―――――――――

Mayor Bill Welch

June 11, 1995

**12:30 am**
At the Allen Street Grill,
Kelly Hale and Keith
Wagner are on their
first date.

*Cathy Seith*

**12:41 am**
Nittany Lion paw prints
painted on the pavement
lead to the Student
Book Store.

*H. A. Rader*

**1:10 am**
John Cecco, press operator, inspects the print quality of
the *Centre Daily Times*. The CDT has chronicled State
College since its presses started in 1898, just two years
after the incorporation of the borough itself.

*Cathy Seith*

**1:15 am**

The heart of our town is where College crosses Allen.
Since before the turn of the century, this eastern corner
has been the site of small businesses, each of which
contributed to the charm of the downtown in its day.
Graham's News and Tobacco originated here in 1896.
Later came the Athletic Store, which sold, among other
things, textbooks that clerks "delivered" to customers by
throwing them from the storage area to the front counter.
Moyer Jewelers moved to this corner in 1975.

*H. A. Rader*

**1:18 am**

Since its beginnings as James Jack's Roadhouse in 1855, the Hotel State College has been the cornerstone of the downtown. Its history is the town's history. It was the setting of many "firsts," including: the first hotel, the first horse and buggy stop, the first telephone hookup, and the first Western Union connection.

*H. A. Rader*

**2:00 am**

Open twenty-four hours a day, every day of the year, Ye Olde College Diner & Bakery caters to night owls. Among the patrons this night are (clockwise from top left): Matt Schaefer, Kristi Molyneaux, Mark Ginter, and Chuck Schaefer. The Diner was established in 1929 and is famed for its grilled stickies. Patrons who were around when it was the "New College Diner" still call it the "NCD."

*Cathy Seith*

**3:30 am**
Frank Talamo tends the register at Boots Dairyette. Despite changes in ownership and appearance over the years, Boots Dairyette remains essentially the same as it was when Rufus "Boots" Ripka opened it in 1959 as a corner grocery store serving the neighborhood around Beaver and Atherton.

*H. A. Rader*

**2:45 am**
Penn State graduate Jason Cassady works at Bi Lo Food Market while awaiting the start of a job in his field.

*H. A. Rader*

**5:45 am**
Carpenter Randy Neff begins his shift at the construction site for the Bryce Jordan Center.

*Eugene W. Moon*

**6:00 am**

The Pugh Street Parking Garage, the borough's first multilevel parking structure, opened on Valentine's Day 1972.

*H. A. Rader*

**6:05 am**

Once the site of the jail and the fire company, 118 South Fraser is now the State College Municipal Building, which houses administrative offices and the police department. Here is where residents come to pay their parking tickets and their taxes, to attend borough council meetings, and to see the mayor.

*H. A. Rader*

**6:15 am**

Legend has it that Indian maiden Ni-Ta-Nee once lived in this valley and gave her name to the mountain beloved by all who hold State College dear — Mount Nittany.

*Denny Kaltreider*

**6:35 am**

If you build it, they will come. The Bryce Jordan Center at Penn State is a multipurpose arena slated to open in the year of the State College Centennial—1996.

*Steve Williams*

**6:45 am**

Sunrise over State College as seen from the photographer's backyard in Park Hills.

*Roger Pennock, Jr.*

**6:55 am**

Now Pennsylvania's sixth-busiest airport, the University Park Airport had quaint beginnings as a rural airstrip where a mobile home served as its terminal.

*Howard P. Nuernberger*

**7:12 am**

Lab technician Lewis Brown walks along the tanks of the Penn State Waste Water Treatment Plant on University Drive, which treats about half of the borough's waste.

*Philip I. Park*

**7:00 am**

State High seniors Marie Barrickman and Katy Rowley wait for the school bus.

*Scott Elmquist*

**7:03 am**

Superintendent of streets and sewers Dick Waltz, a borough employee since 1955, arrives for work.

*Peter S. Marshall*

**7:14 am**
On Penfield Road, Lurene Frantz, Virginia Labenski, and Joyce Moon take their usual morning walk.

*Scott Elmquist*

**7:25 am**
Morning sun drenches the Penn State Research Park as Earl Ivory rolls on a coat of paint.

*Alice E. Clark*

**7:15 am**
Sheep graze in the fields by Centre Community Hospital.

*Scott Flohr*

**7:26 am**
Centre Region Parks and Recreation supervisor Greg Roth and Public Works employees Carl Reynolds and Dair Rider, Jr., are about to begin their workday.

*Peter S. Marshall*

**7:27 am**

Cook Nathan Collamer
scrambles eggs for an
"Early Bird Special" — a
popular breakfast platter at
the Corner Room.

*Heather McDermott*

**7:30 am**

Bernie McCue, Penn State
Math Center coordinator,
is a breakfast regular at the
Corner Room.

*Heather McDermott*

**7:30 am**

At Harner Farms, seasonal employee Randy Dick helps with the harvest.

*Stacie Bird*

**7:32 am**

The landscaped McAllister Alley provides a pedestrian walkway between College Avenue and Calder Way.

*Ronald A. Davis*

**7:34 am**

Like this angler, many State College residents enjoy fishing, boating, hiking, and picnicking at the Stone Valley Recreation Area of Penn State.

*Denise Wagner*

**7:45 am**

Patricia Yackley, staff assistant for PENNTAP, scans the sports section of the *Centre Daily Times*.

*Alice E. Clark*

(Above, left) Three-year-old Maxwell Weiss, left, enjoys waiting for the school bus which takes his brother Lucien, 6, neighbor Daniel Collins, 6, and eldest brother Walter, 8, to the Friends School.

*James Collins*

**7:45 am**

(Above) Traffic streams along the stretch of Westerly Parkway that bisects the north and south campuses of State High.

*Robert M. Baumbach*

**7:50 am**

In College Heights, Claudine Nuernberger gives her garage door a facelift.

*John Bellanti*

**8:00 am**

Electrician Daniel Rivera tests a landing guidance system for pilots as part of the preventive-maintenance schedule at University Park Airport.

*Howard P. Nuernberger*

**8:00 am**

To signify the start of their "duty" day, members of the Penn State Air Force ROTC color guard unfurl the U.S. and P.O.W. flags at Wagner Building.

*Cathy Seith*

**8:10 am**

In Nittany Hills, working mom Robin Bagby assures her daughter, Julia, a kindergarten student, that her very first ride on the school bus will be fun.

*Mary Lou Snitger*

**8:15 am**

Crossing guard Maya Izakov is on patrol across the street from Fairmount Avenue Elementary School.

*Norma Keller*

**8:16 am**

Chris Collier and Ruchi Bhatia are among the students arriving at Fairmount Avenue Elementary School. Two hundred children, representing twenty-eight countries, attend kindergarten through sixth grade there.

*Norma Keller*

**8:30 am**

Bob Butler, a Penn State retiree, who now works as an artist and a community volunteer in the arts, rides along the fitness trail at Toftrees. In recent years, State College has received national notoriety as a haven for retirees because of the pleasant quality of life here.

*Lois R. Chavern*

**8:31 am**

Seniors Stacey Martilotta, Jenna Kiel, and Tracy Stocker are in study hall at State High.

*Robert M. Baumbach*

**8:50 am**

Deanna Yarnell and Joyce Lewis, executive secretaries at HRB Systems, pause from their paperwork for a portrait by the company's resident photographer who, on this day, is doubling as a Centennial photographer.

*Richard S. Orr*

**8:50 am**

Assistant professor Jock Lauterer's Penn State photojournalism students check their cameras before dispersing to photograph State College as a class assignment.

*Jock Lauterer*

**9:00 am**

Maria Novak Mooney and her daughter, Mikaela, are poolside awaiting the start of the water aerobics class at The Athletic Club.

*Rita Foderaro*

**9:00 am**

At Our Lady of Victory Catholic Church, Monsignor Philip Saylor says mass.

*Carolyn Clinefelter Smith*

**9:08 am**

Robert J. Price is executive director of Downtown State College, an organization that promotes the vitality of the business district through the cooperative efforts of merchants, the borough, and Penn State.

*Steve Welch*

**9:15 am**
At HRB Systems, a company that provides technology for the U.S. intelligence community, Frieda Johns assembles a printed circuit board.

*Richard S. Orr*

**9:15 am**
Ninety-year-old Carl Harpster, a lifelong resident of State College, waits for the bus to take him downtown to pay his phone bill and to do other errands.

*Scott Elmquist*

**9:30 am**
Roger Ishler, a carpenter with Bosak Construction, works atop a new house at Teaberry Ridge.

*Bill Wallace*

**9:35 am**
Bill Harris, a machinist at HRB Systems, mills a housing.

*Richard S. Orr*

**9:40 am**
Penn State landscape architecture students sketch by the pond at Toftrees.

*James R. DeTuerk*

**9:40 am**
At State High, a drafting class is in session.

*Brian Hill*

**10:00 am**
(Below) The twelve hundred block of West College Avenue features a row of mail-order bungalows built in the 1920s.

*Li Chen*

**9:40 am**
Barry L. Belinda, instrument and meter technician, climbs the stack of the West Campus Steam Plant at Penn State to check the pollution control system.

*Richard L. Crowley*

**10:00 am**

A natural depression that old timers colloquially call "The Hollow," Memorial Field is the gridiron for the State College Little Lions. In the summer, the stadium serves as an amphitheater for the Central Pennsylvania Festival of the Arts.

*Norma Keller*

**10:00 am**

Brian Spear paints a home on McKee Street.

*Scott Elmquist*

**10:15 am**

The Meyer Dairy Farm borders scenic West Branch
Road. Established on a few acres in 1887, Meyer Dairy
Farms now stretch across six separate sites for a total of
1,000 acres and are operated by the Joe Meyer family,
third-generation owners.

*Steve Williams*

**10:17 am**

F. J. Gutierrez participates in Zesty Chair Exercises at the Centre Region Senior Center.

*Raegan Owens*

**10:28 am**

Julie Buron, Mitra Arjmand, and Nila Nanavati confer about the chemistry of a solution at Centre Analytical Laboratories.

*David S. Palermo*

**10:30 am**

Thanks to Ronald Kresge's daily diligence, the storefront of Bostonian Ltd. always sparkles.

*Mary Lou Snitger*

**10:30 am**
At Lemont Elementary
School, Judy Strayer's
second graders gather to
sing their club song:
"We're all together again
on a Monday morning
after a long weekend!"

*Judy Strayer*

**10:35 am**
Second grader Trevor
Muffley builds his strength
in Phys Ed class at Lemont
Elementary School.
Teacher Judy Strayer took
a camera to school so that
her students could
photograph each other.

*Eric Smith, age 7*

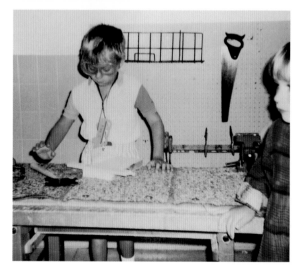

**10:38 am**
Nothing can break the
concentration of kindergarten student Alex Cross as
he works in the "shop" at
Lemont Elementary School
— not even being photo-
graphed by his
"paparazzo" classmate.
Teacher Linda Domin
provided a camera for her
students to record the day's
activities.

*Sean Zembower, age 6*

**10:40 am**
The Toddler Parade is a daily sight in downtown State College. This group, led by care givers Hannah Wilson and Brenda Hopkins, is from the Penn State Office of Human Resources' Child Care Center, which is based at St. Paul's United Methodist Church. The center serves Penn State families.

*Robert J. Price*

**10:45 am**

Bob Herrold of West Penn Power works at the site of the former G. C. Murphy Company as it undergoes a conversion to Chili's Grill & Bar and the Eddie Bauer clothing store.

*Steve Williams*

**10:54 am**

In six minutes, the bell tower of Old Main will ring out with the hourly Westminster chimes.

*Kim Winck*

**11:00 am**

Friends meet for coffee
and conversation at the
Daily Grind.

*Marc B. Levey*

**11:00 am**

Judi Kur conducts kindergarten at Radio Park Elementary School.

*Carolyn Clinefelter Smith*

**11:05 am**

Ann Van Kuren is artistic director of the Pennsylvania
Dance Theatre, a professional modern dance company
that bills itself as "a national treasure right here at home."
This morning, she is developing choreography to be
performed in collaboration with the Nittany Valley
Symphony.

*Helena Lukas Martemucci*

**11:10 am**

On South Allen Street, the mural - "Our World" - camoflauges the empty lot where McLanahan's burned down in 1989. In 1993, under the auspices of the Central Pennsylvania Festival of the Arts, New York artist Maria Cochiarelli and art-camp students from the Hetzel Union Center for Arts and Crafts collaborated to create and paint the mural on site.

*Marc B. Levey*

**11:10 am**

Steve Williams prepares to photograph State College Mayor Emeritus Arnold Addison who is the Chairman of the State College Centennial Commission.

*Pat Little*

**11:15 am**

The mayor emeritus, who has served the borough as an elected official for one-third of its existence, stands profiled against Addison Court. The apartment building named for him is the first major public/private partnership enterprise in the borough. Addison Court provides its residents, many of them senior citizens, with affordable and convenient downtown living.

*Steve Williams*

**11:23 am**
Stephen Shirey and Wayne Perkins, dendricians with the State College Public Works Department, tidy up one of many floral islands that the borough has incorporated into its street designs. The borough's commitment to greenery dates back to 1903 when the borough council adopted an ordinance for the upkeep of trees — an act that accounts for the many mature trees that line our neighborhoods. For its active tree planting and maintenance program and for its community outreach about the value of trees, the borough has been designated a "Tree City USA" by the National Arbor Day Foundation every year since 1984.

*Marion R. Deppen*

**11:30 am**
Carver Nelson Wood nears completion on the Centennial plaque, based on the logo design by Cheryl Weisz.

*Lois R. Chavern*

**11:30 am**
Stephanie Gush arranges a harvest display at Harner Farms Market.

*John C. Flohr*

**11:36 am**
At Easterly Parkway Elementary School, fifth graders Kelli and Trea enjoy recess.

*Charles A. Fitzgerald*

**11:40 am**
The intersection of Beaver and Allen from a driver's point of view

*Pat Little*

**11:45 am**
Penn State senior Chris Naugle studies outside because he wants to "enjoy the weather before it gets too cold."

*Michael T. Jesky*

**11:45 am**

At Tower of Glass, loyal shop dog, Tona Bell Gong Sri, keeps owner Andrea Minasian company and on occasion entertains customers with his repertoire of tricks.

*John Dickison*

**11:55 am**

Wayne Gersie, a Penn State junior from New York City, reads his mail outside the State College Post Office.

*Pat Little*

**12:00 pm**

A State College landmark strikes high noon. This clock still stands on South Allen Street thanks to the foresight of Dr. H. Richard Ishler. In the late 1960s, in its present site, Peoples National Bank had its building demolished and replaced with a modern one. The clock, a landmark even then, was expected to be torn down since the new building design incorporated a streetside time and temperature sign. Amidst the demolition, Dr. Ishler, a board member of the bank, arranged for the clock's face and works to be stored at a nearby farm simply to preserve it as a historical artifact. As the new building neared completion, however, bank officials discovered that local ordinances prohibited the placement of the new time and temperature sign. But the ordinances did allow for the old clock to be rebuilt and replaced in its original position — where it remains today. Though People's National Bank has since become Omega Bank, the clock will stay a part of the downtown landscape.

*Charles A. Fitzgerald*

**12:00 pm**
Construction continues
on the State College
Presbyterian Church
addition, which will house
a choir room, a preschool,
and classrooms for
religious instruction and
youth programs.

*Don Werb*

**12:01 pm**
(Above) "Meet me
at the Corner!"

*I. Jeanne Miller*

**12:05 pm**
The rear of 225 South
Burrowes Street typifies
the narrow, deep back-
yards of old State College.

*Edward Leos*

**12:04 pm**
Thousands cross College Avenue daily at the gates
of the Old Main Mall.

*James R. DeTuerk*

**12:10 pm**
James A. Moss, president
and publisher of the
*Centre Daily Times*, says that
this area is, "a vital and
exciting place to publish a
newspaper. Chronicling
the daily history of a
community like this is a
dream-come-true."

*Steve Tressler*

**12:15 pm**

A cluster of bikes gives curbside appeal to the Bicycle Shop on West College Avenue.

*Brian Hill*

**12:20 pm**

This stained glass window is one of many designed into the architecture of St. Paul's United Methodist Church.

*Charles A. Fitzgerald*

**12:30 pm**

At the Red Satchel Montessori Preschool, Julia Brewer, Wes Showalter, and Sean Bradley sort building blocks.

*Stephanie Seraydarian*

**12:32 pm**
Motorists take advantage of the drive-by mail boxes on South Fraser Street.

*Edward Leos*

**12:35 pm**
Carol Dillon and Amy Gette, secretaries with the law offices of Richard L. Kalin and H. Denning Mason, have lunch in the office and continue to answer phones while watching their favorite soap opera: "The Young and the Restless."

*Pat Little*

**12:40 pm**
Matt Corl helps his father, Gene, with the haying at Heart's Desire Holsteins, at the junction of Routes 26 and 45.

*Mary Sue Henszey*

**12:48 pm**
At the meat counter of O. W. Houts & Son, manager Chris Kuhn waits on a customer.

*Russell V. Meyers*

**12:49 pm**

At Truly Yours, a greeting card gallery, owner Mary Jane Schiavo prepares balloon bouquets for the Balloon Baboon and other costumed creatures who deliver goodies and greetings, often with a song.

*Pat Little*

**12:55 pm**

Students sketch on the plaza of the Palmer Museum of Art at Penn State.

*Richard L. Crowley*

**12:57 pm**

Louise Mott, a 102-year-old resident of the Inn at Brookline Village, says of her longevity, "I used to eat a lot of cookies and candies. I eat what I like. Maybe that's my secret!" Appropriately, Louise is known for her dangerously delicious fudge recipe.

*Raegan Owens*

**1:00 pm**

(Top) Newt, a stray cat that the photographer adopted, signals that she wants to wander outside for awhile.

*Li Chen*

**1:00 pm**

(Bottom) Using a molecular model, Penn State student Indira Belizaire studies for a science exam at the Paul Robeson Cultural Center.

*Marian Cannon Dornell*

**1:05 pm**
Clothes dance on the wash line in this scene along the Benner Pike.
*Lois Todd*

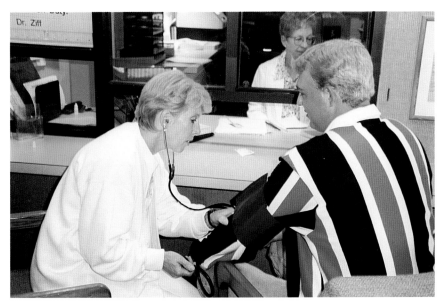

**1:07 pm**
At Centre Community Hospital's Emergency Department, Darlene Zweig, R.N., and Sherry Moyer of admissions attend to Penn State student Alan Strand.

*Donna F. Williams*

**1:15 pm**
"The Wall" along College Avenue lures passersby to its tranquility.

*Alan John Sidwar*

**1:20 pm**

U.S. Postal Service letter carrier Carmine Dinello is on his rounds in the downtown.

*Alan John Sidwar*

**1:20 pm**

Construction on Route 26 stalled the photographer in traffic and provided this photo opportunity.

*Li Chen*

**1:22 pm**

Alfalfa is delivered to the "original" Penn State Horse Barn, which protects horses especially during periods of severe weather. The barn, across the street from Beaver Stadium, was constructed, in part, with the wooden bleachers from the university's first stadium.

*Denise Wagner*

Harry Heidi Joe Joel Sonya
Mrs. Linder Mrs. Pearson Mrs. Greene

**1:30 pm**

On South Allen Street, Norah Philbin uses the Omega Bank MAC Machine.

*John Dickison*

**1:50 pm**

Wanting to develop their social skills by mingling with peers, the "Wild Dream Team" chose as the site for their LifeLink Lab an apartment complex which houses Penn State students. Relaxing in the clubroom of their apartment complex are Matt Campbell, Jessyca Hogan, and Jeff Fredericks.

*Kim Dionis*

**1:45 pm**

The "Wild Dream Team" members show off a van with a wheel-chair lift that they bought for the local Easter Seal Society. The van, which has team members' names on it, was bought with the $15,000 they earned as winners of a Paul Newman recipe contest. The team includes: (front row, from left) Teri Lindner, learning support teacher; Erin Scanlon; Cristin McTavish; Jessyca Hogan; and Sharon Pearson, assistant learning support teacher. Back row, from left: Sonya Greene, sign language interpreter; Chris Dixon; Matt Prosek; Jeff Fredericks; Leonard Hockenberry; and Matt Campbell.

"Wild Dream Team" members are special needs students who thought up the idea of gaining experience outside of the classroom by living in an apartment in town. At their apartment, which is called the LifeLink Lab, the students live for extended periods of time with transition coaches. While there, they learn how to cook, clean, do laundry, and handle a budget. The LifeLink Lab is new to the high school this year and is the first of its kind in the United States.

*Kim Dionis*

The photographer, a nature lover, framed this version of the Penn State Nittany Lion Shrine because it "reminds me of being on a walk in the woods."

*Kathy D. Long*

**2:00 pm**
Deanna Walden-Turek, the first baby born at Centre Community Hospital September 12, 1994, is admired by her parents, Daniel and Ruth.

*Cathy Seith*

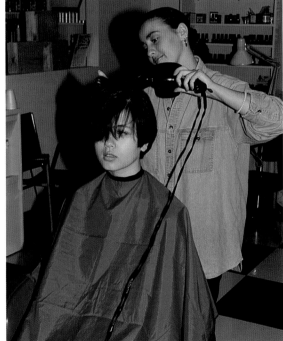

**2:00 pm**
At Looks Hair Design, stylist Lisa Hughes shapes a new hairdo for Lisa Keller.

*Alice E. Clark*

**2:00 pm**
Clara Corl of Pine Grove Road, "Grandma Corl" to the photographer, is descibed as a dear family friend who quilts and gardens and is "a lot younger than her age" of ninety-four years.

*Tonya Lynn Martin*

**2:00 pm**

The photographer, a State High junior, created this image at school while working on an assignment for teacher Bob Baumbach's Photography II course.

*Nova Ritchey*

**2:05 pm**

Gregarious Edna Lyons and Shirley Yearick delight in having their picture taken together. They are members of the residential program of the Association for Retarded Citizens. Edna especially enjoys visiting the Senior Citizens Center and shopping at the mall. Shirley likes to take walks and is a devotee of the "Lawrence Welk Show."

*Raegan Owens*

**2:01 pm**

Betty Jean Homan speaks to the photographer in sign language. She is a participant in the residential program of the Association for Retarded Citizens. Among Betty Jean's favorite pastimes is tenting with her family at the Grange Fair.

*Raegan Owens*

**2:06 pm**

Fraser Street Plaza

*Pat Little*

**2:10 pm**

Leap of Faith! In-line skater Pat Kirkham jumps the steps outside Willard Building.

*Arthur Boller*

**2:15 pm**

Geoffrey May, a construction laborer, fills a concrete bucket to pour columns for the Bryce Jordan Center.

*Erman M. Moon*

**2:17 pm**

Kindergarten students Ryan Watson, Ben Jones, and William Spicer listen to stories at Lemont Elementary School. The photographer says, "Mrs. Domin, my teacher, gave me the camera and told me to take any picture I wanted to."

*Adam Bergeman, age 6*

**2:20 pm**

Construction worker John Howard helps with the surveying for the Science Park Road relocation project.

*Tonya Lynn Martin*

**2:25 pm**

Charles Petnick, his daughter, Charlene Petnick Rosen, and her dog, Sasha, stand outside the Mr. Charles Shop, one of several dress boutiques in the downtown. Charles Petnick founded the shop fifty-three years ago and today runs the business with his daughter and son, Nick (not shown).

*Chuck Mong*

**2:25 pm**
A view of Beaver Stadium
from the cow barns

*Charles A. Fitzgerald*

**2:30 pm**

Looking eastward from atop the Fraser Street Parking Garage, the photographer discovered workers renovating the rooftop of the old G. C. Murphy building for its new occupants, Eddie Bauer and Chili's.

*Robert L. Fantauzzo*

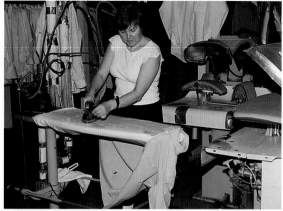

**2:30 pm**

(Top) Tatyana Achapkin presses a shirt at Balfurd Dry Cleaners. Tatyana came to State College in 1992 from Almaty, Kazakhstan (formerly the USSR).

*Alice E. Clark*

**2:40 pm**

(Bottom) Beth Gardner, a graduate student, checks for honey at a Penn State apiary.

*Denise Wagner*

**2:43 pm**
In Old Main, Joab Thomas, the fifteenth president of The Pennsylvania State University, prepares for his next meeting. President Thomas made as his mission of leadership a focus on undergraduate education and an aggressive campus building campaign.

*Richard L. Crowley*

**2:45 pm**
At a Penn State graduate housing complex, one of a group of children gets some special attention from the care giver.

*Lois Todd*

**2:45 pm**
Certified optician Bob Nace makes a few adjustments. He especially enjoys fitting people with their first pair of glasses because, he says, they often exclaim, "I didn't know what I was missing!"

*Denny Kaltreider*

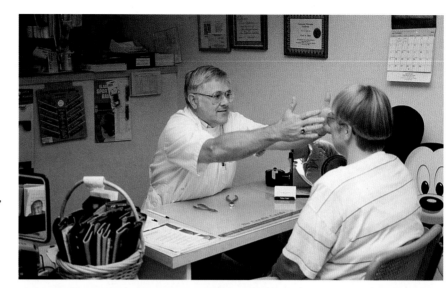

**3:00 pm**
Brian Eagon, Penn State assistant horse herd manager, handles Clue Express, a three-year-old quarter horse.

*Tonya Lynn Martin*

**3:00 pm**

Hal Hallock and his metalflake lavender 1958 Corvette are a familiar duo around town. Hal is an actor, artist, art teacher with the State College Area School District, and a devoted Harley-Davidson motorcyclist.

*Denny Kaltreider*

**3:00 pm**

Amused, the photographer entitled this image "The Dilemma."

*Christine E. Wilson*

**3:00 pm**

Storefront signage on College Avenue

*Clarissa I. González*

**3:00 pm**

Rooftops to the northeast of the Fraser Street Parking Garage are evidence that State College "is becoming a metropolitan area and that its skyline is changing accordingly," says the photographer.

*Arthur Beward*

**3:00 pm**

Teacher Mark Smeal took this picture of his third-grade students at Houserville Elementary School "to capture the essence of a typical end-of-day for most school students."

*Mark Smeal*

**3:03 pm**

(Left) Coffee break at Café Gourmet

*David S. Palermo*

**3:05 pm**

Joyce Moon, a volunteer with Downtown State College, organizes a display of Centre County brochures. Tourism brings brisk business to this town year-round.

*Steve Welch*

**3:10 pm**
State High sweethearts
Chip Taylor and Annie
Cucuel kiss good-bye
after school.

*Cathy Seith*

**3:22 pm**
At Mount Nittany Vineyard and Winery, owners Betty
and Joe Carroll use a refractometer to measure the sugar
content of grapes to help them determine when the
harvest should begin. Situated on the southern slope of
Mount Nittany above Linden Hall, the vineyard has an
ideal microclimate for growing premium grapes.

*Russell V. Meyers*

**3:30 pm**
Hoop it up! The photogra-
pher says this picture
really captures her son,
Daniel: "He's an exuberant
kid who loves to shoot
baskets after school."

*Sue P. LaBrecque*

**3:30 pm**

Officer Joseph S. Grego, an eleven-year veteran of the State College Police Department, investigates a collision on College Avenue. The size of State College, he says, appeals to him as an officer and family man.

*Maryann Curione*

**3:30 pm**

Penn State students Lalynn Nock and Scott Thalman relax on Old Main Lawn.

*Julie L. Nash*

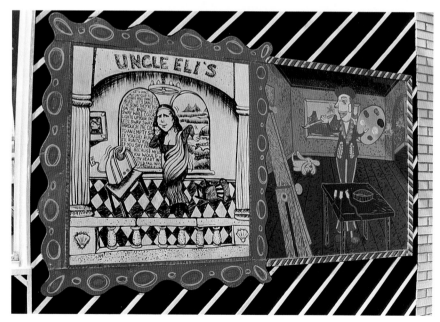

**3:30 pm**

The storefront of Uncle Eli's includes eclectic window displays and this adjoining mural.

*Norma Keller*

**3:30 pm**

The Centre County Library Bookmobile visits Lemont. Every two weeks the Bookmobile makes more than seventy scheduled stops throughout the Centre Region.

*Barbara J. Kasales*

**3:30 pm**
Nadine Kofman looks up from a script she is reading as a member of the State College Community Theatre play-selection committee. The local columnist and writer is known for her folksy articles about this community and about her lovable cats. She is married to Mayor Bill Welch.

*Anne Quinn Corr*

**3:30 pm**
In a J-V game at Memorial Field, the State College Little Lions fight their way to a 13-7 win over Hollidaysburg.

*Jay C. Mastalerz*

**3:30 pm**
Wendy Branstetter, Phil Hampt, Donna Graves, and Marsha Sallurday leave work as the shift changes at Murata Electronics.

*Paul D. Ruby*

**3:30 pm**
"Pictasaurus," by artist John Parker, distinguishes Fraser Street Plaza. It was presented to the borough in 1986 by the Art in Public Places Committee of the Central Pennsylvania Festival of the Arts.

*Ronald A. Davis*

**3:31 pm**

Twelve hundred tons of rugged mountain stone were used to build Grace Lutheran Church in 1965. Incorporated in 1898, Grace Lutheran occupied several downtown sites before moving to the knoll at East Beaver and South Garner — a site carefully chosen to hold with the church's mission of serving the community and the university.

*Cecil & Doris Trueblood*

**3:40 pm**

(Top right) Eva Marciaone and her daughter, Sara, buy provisions at the Meyer Dairy Store.

*Tonya Lynn Martin*

**3:45 pm**

The Penn State Lady Lion Softball Team practices fielding.

*Mark Selders*

**3:45 pm**

(Above) John Drummond, of the Raptor Center at Shaver's Creek, hand-feeds Butey, a blind 14-year-old red-tailed hawk. Butey is one of many injured, nonreleasable birds of prey used for breeding rare species. Many State College students learn about nature by taking field trips to Shaver's Creek Environmental Center.

*Mary Sue Henszey*

**3:45 pm**

Depending on your perspective, The Tavern is a restaurant-in-a-gallery or a gallery-in-a-restaurant. Either way, The Tavern Restaurant means tradition. For nearly half a century, The Tavern has provided its patrons with an extensive display of period prints and photographs about Pennsylvania and State College, including images that document its own centrality to town history.

*Cecil & Doris Trueblood*

**3:50 pm**

Established in the early 1960s, the Synagogue of Congregation Brit Shalom on East Hamilton Avenue serves the Jewish community of the State College/Bellefonte area. It offers worship services, Sunday school, and cultural activities for its members.

*Annette Shirey McHugh*

**3:51 pm**

(Top right) Classes change at Penn State.

*Richard L. Crowley*

**3:53 pm**

On the patio of Penn State's School of Music, cellist Jason Majewski, a music performance major who prefers practicing outdoors, plays a movement from the Sonata in E Minor by Brahms, in preparation for a recital.

*James R. DeTuerk*

**4:00 pm**
State High cheerleaders perfect their routines.

*Carolyn Clinefelter Smith*

**4:00 pm**
Nicholas Wyckoff works out with playground equipment in the pre-school program of the Easter Seal Society.

*Norma Keller*

**4:00 pm**
The suburbs of State College are booming with new housing starts and commercial development. Typical of this growth is the recent opening of Lowe's Home Improvement Center, where Darlene Rogers helps customer Chris Spicer.

*Donna M. Neufer*

**4:00 pm**
The patio of Café 210 West is popular for its leisurely atmosphere.

*Jennifer Whittaker*

**4:18 pm**
(Above) Matt Homan with Orphan the cow

*Stacie Bird*

**4:15 pm**
Claude, Matt, and Joe Homan (as well as Captain the cat and Lucy the dog) are a farming family in Ferguson Township.

*Stacie Bird*

**4:20 pm**
Dan Hawbaker, owner of Glenn O. Hawbaker Construction Company, and Dean McKnight, senior vice president of Mid-State Bank, discuss a road improvement project.

*Chuck Mong*

**4:30 pm**
(Far left) Centre County district attorney Ray Gricar returns a serve at the community tennis courts on West Prospect Avenue.

*Jay C. Mastalerz*

**4:30 pm**
Four-year-old April Frank plays in one of those ubiquitous turtle sand boxes.

*Drew C. Frank*

**4:30 pm**
At Appliance World, owner and master repairman, David Zeligman, awaits more broken blenders. Started in 1979, Appliance World is a veritable supermarket of parts for new or even "antique" household gadgets.

*Ralph Fearing*

**4:37 pm**
Kay McKnight walks
Rafferty, Finn McCool,
and Annie Murphy along
Outer Drive.

*Denny Kaltreider*

**4:40 pm**
At Penn State, Myrna
Munchus-Bullock teaches
a course in African dance
and culture.

*Helena Lukas Martemucci*

**4:45 pm**
Many early residents of State College are buried in Pine
Hall Cemetery, which is shared by St. Peter's United
Church of Christ (shown in the background) and Pine
Hall Lutheran Church. The churches stand across the
street from each other on West College Avenue.

*Charles A. Fitzgerald*

**4:50 pm**

The All American Rathskeller, commonly called "The Skeller," occupies the basement of State College's oldest apartment building, which dates back to 1894.

*Roger Pennock, Jr.*

**5:00 pm**

Schlow Memorial Library is a magnet in downtown State College, drawing about 1,000 visitors daily, who, in a year, check out nearly a half a million items! To patrons, the library is more than a repository; it is a community center. Students do homework here, researchers huddle over computers, chess players drop in for an impromptu game, families gather for "Storytime," local artists hang exhibits in the gallery, interest groups convene in the meeting room, and the regulars read newspapers from their favorite chairs.

*Ralph Fearing*

**5:05 pm**
At University Park Airport, commuters en route to Philadelphia board USAir Express.

*Howard P. Nuernberger*

**5:10 pm**
State College real estate developer Sidney Friedman has greatly influenced the look and the feel of State College, especially in the downtown business district.

*Steve Williams*

**5:15 pm**
The Boal Barn Playhouse is the summer stage for the State College Community Theatre.

*John C. Flohr*

**5:20 pm**

Having taken off from University Park Airport, Robert T. Sherwood flies his Cessna Skyhawk above town so that his wife, Ellen, can photograph the local terrain.

*Ellen M. Sherwood*

**5:20 pm**

Sam Ricciotti and John Torres, officers with the Penn State Police Services Bicycle Patrol, are ready to go on duty.

*Ellen J. Aschenbrenner*

**5:30 pm**

Three-and-a-half-year-old Sammy Meister, self-appointed campus police officer, tries to arrest Penn State students on the steps of Pattee Library.

*Michele Polignone*

**5:30 pm**

Golfers Nancy and Glenn Gamble are on the tenth green at Centre Hills Country Club.

*Lois R. Chavern*

**5:35 pm**

The Land of Oz is in Oak Hall. Drive along Linden Hall Road and you will encounter these four at Smithanson Acres — the homestead of Stan and Darlene Smith. The Smiths, helped by other family members, built the grouping one by one over several years from scraps donated or found. What began as a lark has become a tradition that they plan to continue by periodically introducing new characters.

*Kim N. Fisher*

**5:47 pm**
Established in 1977 by Marie Librizzi and Janet McKenna, the Old Main Frame Shop & Gallery is one of many locally-owned specialty shops that make our downtown unique.

*Elizabeth H. Pennock*

**5:44 pm**
Susan Beyerle and her daughter, Laura, try a slide at Holmes-Foster Park, one of twelve parks in the borough.

*David E. Beyerle*

**5:45 pm**
Nancy and Glenn Gamble wind their way along the back nine at Centre Hills Country Club, a course that, true to its name, challenges golfers from tee to green with its hilly contour.

*Lois R. Chavern*

**5:50 pm**

The Penn State Blue Band struts its stuff.

*Drew C. Frank*

**5:52 pm**

The photographer says that this scene along East College Avenue is born of her love of strolling and shopping in the downtown, "a pedestrian's paradise."

*Elizabeth H. Pennock*

**6:00 pm**

Penn State students Chrissa Pullicino, Alison Scott, and Kelly Polizzi are on their way to a sorority rush party.

*Matthew F. Brashears*

**6:00 pm**

Loved by the locals, O. W. Houts and Son has been a tradition in State College since 1920. According to its own brochure, Houts sells "everything to build, furnish, and maintain your home." Where else can you buy fresh seafood, fine china, faucets, furniture, Formica, fertilizer, and flowers?

*Ralph Fearing*

**6:00 pm**

Distinctive in its brickwork, arches, and tiled roof, this building, designed by State College architect P. Boyd Kapp in the early 1920s, has been home to three barber shops. In 1925, barber George Smith set up shop on the main floor while his wife ran The Powder Puff, a beauty shop, upstairs. Next came Rinaldo's Barber Shop. The third and current owner, Wayne Britten, kept the name Rinaldo's when he bought the shop in 1987 because he says, "It sounds barbershoppy."

*Elizabeth H. Pennock*

**6:00 pm**

As the shutter snaps, Saige Elizabeth Beal Sommese is 8 months, 3 weeks, 3 days, 6 hours, and 45 minutes old.

*Kristin Breslin Sommese*

**6:01 pm**

Joe Paterno, head football coach of the Penn State Nittany Lions for twenty-nine years, conducts practice early in what would become a historic, undefeated season, culminating in Big Ten and Rose Bowl Championships. Coach Paterno is the nation's leading active coach in victories.

*Cathy Seith*

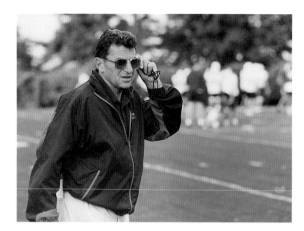

**6:09 pm**

With Mount Nittany as the backdrop, the Nittany Lions scrimmage on the practice field near Holuba Hall.

*Mark Selders*

**6:15 pm**

Maryann Curione photographs the Alpha Fire Company as it responds to the alarm at the Armenara Plaza Apartments on East Beaver Avenue.

*Cathy Seith*

**6:15 pm**

On the scene is Todd Gibney, firefighter with the Alpha Fire Company. The call was soon determined to be a false alarm.

*Maryann Curione*

**6:10 pm**

Residents of Beaver Terrace Apartments watch as fire trucks approach the building across the street.

*Cathy Seith*

**6:17 pm**

John Woika tends to plantings at his Park Forest Village home.

*David S. Palermo*

**6:20 pm**

Beth Beatty visits her neighbor's goats at Slab Cabin Farm on Route 45.

*Tonya Lynn Martin*

**6:20 pm**

Dr. Marcus H. Voth checks the console of the Penn State Breazeale Nuclear Reactor, the longest operating university research reactor in the United States. The reactor provides neutrons for researchers throughout the Commonwealth.

*Clarence D. Johnson, Jr.*

**6:25 pm**

Established in 1957 by Guy V. Kresge, Bostonian Ltd. is one of several longstanding family-run businesses in the borough.

*Cecil & Doris Trueblood*

**6:30 pm**

A view of Centre Hills Country Club and beyond includes a pool where many State College children learn to swim.

*Carolyn Clinefelter Smith*

**6:30 pm**

Henry Fong, owner of the Canton Restaurant, accommodates the photographer's request for a portrait and then treats him to sweet and sour pork "on the house."

*H. A. Rader*

**6:30 pm**

This scarecrow guards the Flower Test Gardens at Penn State.

*Mark Selders*

**6:30 pm**

Flags are flying as the Silk Squad of the State College Area High School Marching Band steps through its maneuvers in the school parking lot.

*Jay C. Mastalerz*

**6:30 pm**

At East Coast Health & Fitness, Matt Gerould is spotting for weight lifter Mark Ollin.

*I. Jeanne Miller*

**6:35 pm**

After dinner, Kathy McGregor pedals along the newly extended Westerly Parkway.

*Stephen McGregor*

**6:55 pm**

Wayne Pagani and his son, David, have shared a love of archery since David was two-years-old. The photographer (David's mom) records family activities like this because "children grow and memories fade too quickly."

*Linda J. Pagani*

**7:00 pm**

A view of Mount Nittany
from Beaver Stadium

*Clarence D. Johnson, Jr.*

**7:00 pm**

At Baby's Burgers and Shakes, shift manager Mike Keifer pours over paperwork.

*I. Jeanne Miller*

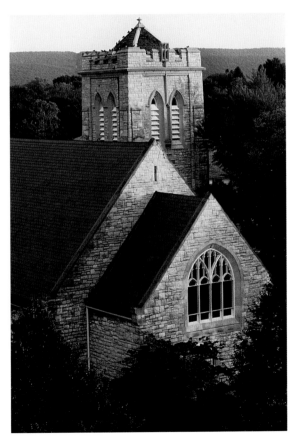

**7:00 pm**

Founded in 1890, the State College Presbyterian Church has been at its present site on East Beaver Avenue since 1913. Though the congregation had once considered moving, the church remains committed to this location because it believes its ministry belongs downtown.

*Cathy Seith*

**7:00 pm**
Elected in November 1993, State College Mayor Bill Welch has lived in the borough for more than fifty years. "State College's great challenge for the next half-century," he says, " is to make our small city as pleasant a place to live and visit as our small town was."

*Steve Tressler*

**7:01 pm**
Gene Shields and his son, Sean, pack it up after fishing awhile at the lake at Stone Valley.

*Pamela A. McHugh*

**7:15 pm**
At Jodon's Stables East, Valerie Puig-Antich, an animal bioscience student at Penn State, exercises and trains Elliot, her thoroughbred.

*Cathy Seith*

**7:15 pm**
Alpha Tau Omega and Fiji (Phi Gamma Delta) fraternities play softball at the Penn State intramural fields.

*Scott Elmquist*

**7:30 pm**

The College Heights Exxon looks much as it did when it first served motorists in 1928. Gary Green, proprietor since 1987, says, "Just about everybody worked here!" Nostalgic Penn State alums and area residents, past and present, often visit to reminisce about pumping gas here decades ago.

*Karen Lintner*

**7:40 pm**

David and Julie Chen established The Golden Wok Restaurant in a brick house on College Avenue in 1983. Since then, they have transformed the decor of the restaurant through major renovations, including the addition of this atrium-like dining room to the front. This kind of architectural metamorphosis is typical of many downtown businesses that originated in what were once early State College homes.

*H. A. Rader*

**7:55 pm**

'Tis the season! A bevy of migrating birds roosts above the parking lot at South Garner Street and Calder Way.

*Li Chen*

**8:05 pm**

Fourth grader Michelle McGregor does her homework in the company of her mom, Debra, and her dog, Pumpkin.

*Stephen McGregor*

**8:10 pm**

The Meyer Dairy Store lights the way for customers who still buy milk in glass bottles.

*Brian Hill*

**8:15 pm**

The photographer, a graphic artist, composed this image at a playground in College Heights because, he says, "In the daytime these creatures appear playful; at night they become surreal. I wondered what they do at night!"

*Lanny Sommese*

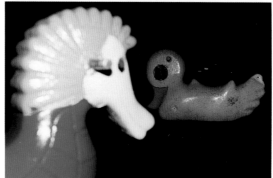

**8:23 pm**

In Park Forest, Scott Morlang takes Megan Overby for a scooter ride.

*Suzanne H. Motley*

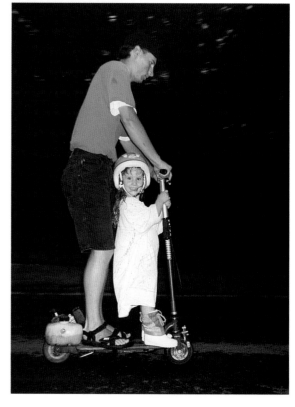

**8:25 pm**
College Avenue

*Scott Flohr*

**8:30 pm**

The Borough Council, the elected policymakers of State College, meets for a work session in the Municipal Building. Among the issues discussed tonight are the borough noise ordinance and the route for a future bike path.
Council members are (from left near the flag): Thomas E. Daubert, Ruth K. Lavin, President Jean W. McManis, R. Thomas Berner, Jerry R. Wettstone, Felicia Lewis, and Janet K. Knauer. Also present is Borough Manager Peter S. Marshall (in the foreground with his back to the camera).

*Steve Williams*

**8:40 pm**

In attendance at the State College Area School Board Meeting are (from left) Evelyn Hall and the Robinson Family — Reginald, mother June, baby Christina, and Terrell.

*Alice E. Clark*

**8:45 pm**

Moonrise over Our Lady of Victory Catholic Church

*Bill Wallace*

**8:40 pm**

Monday nights at the Alpha Fire Station are usually devoted to equipment-maintenance chores and training exercises. Among the crew this evening is Clifford Lutz, Penn State Police Services supervisor, who says that being a volunteer firefighter "requires a lot of mental preparation and a sense of self worth."

*Maryann Curione*

**8:50 pm**

A popular spot for picture-taking, the Jo Hays Vista on Pine Grove Mountain attracted many photographers during these special twenty-four hours. After patiently waiting for nightfall, Mark Selders and Drew C. Frank point their lenses toward the glow of the valley below.

*Rod Fye*

**8:55 pm**

A view of Happy Valley from the Jo Hays Vista

*Mark Selders*

**9:00 pm**
The Nittany Valley Symphony rehearses in the State High auditorium.

*Jay C. Mastalerz*

**9:28 pm**
Baby's Burgers and Shakes, a re-creation of a 1950s diner, is the home of the Teeny-Weeny (a mini ice-cream sundae) and the Wimpy Burger (a pair of hamburgers in a basket). Baby's gained national fame recently when it was featured in an ad campaign for VISA credit cards.

*David S. Palermo*

**9:30 pm**

Mark P. Beach, EMT, is on duty as Crew Chief at Alpha Community Ambulance Service. He describes his job as "very rewarding because people need your help immediately and because you can see the direct results of your efforts. It's a very dynamic type of working lifestyle. You never quite know what you're going to be doing from one shift to another or even from one call to another."

*Maryann Curione*

**9:30 pm**

Thomas R. King, State College chief of police, is responsible for managing the police services for the borough and also for College and Harris Townships. About keeping the peace, he says, "The police can make a difference in this kind of community. Our town is unique because it already has many resources available. We try to improve upon that. We take a proactive approach to problem-solving by working closely with neighborhood associations, the school district, the university, area agencies, and with parents."

*Steve Tressler*

**10:30 pm**

At Café 210 West, "the joint is jumpin" as soundman Dennis Strauser controls the audio mixer during a live musical performace.

*Stephanie Seraydarian*

**10:50 pm**
Pattee Library

*Scott Flohr*

**11:00 pm**

With everything at his fingertips, Penn State senior Hunter Shaw settles in to study finance in his downtown apartment.

*Jennifer Garringer*

**11:10 pm**

At Alpha Sigma Phi Fraternity Paul Garvey, Greg Ott, and Mike Ullrich lounge in a hot tub.

*Matthew L. Garrity*

**11:35 pm**

Amy Balmer bakes bagels at The Bakery on College Avenue.

*John Bellanti*

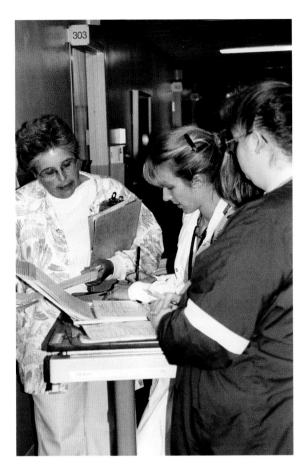

**11:40 pm**
Working the nightshift at Centre Community Hospital, registered nurses Lucinda Saylor, Tracy Withall, and Donna Rowles coordinate patient medications.

*Richard H. Dixon*

**11:50 pm**
On another floor in Centre Community Hospital, Debra Ross, R.N., is in the nursery attending to a newborn.

*Richard H. Dixon*

**11:59 pm**

Under the floodlights of Uni-Mart, John Dickison adds oil to his dying car. Now deceased, the car was a local celebrity because of paraphenalia pasted onto it, including a high-heel shoe and a coffee cup. The car's look was summed up in its vanity plate "No Taste Mobile."

*John Dickison*

## Biographical Sketches

The work of the following 105 photographers appears in this book. We asked them to comment about themselves as photographers and as participants in this project.

**Ellen J. Aschenbrenner** is an officer with Penn State Police Services who worked as the police photographer for the department from 1989 to 1991.
*"I like to take photographs that make me feel good. I like to look at them years after they've been taken and remember the stories behind them."*

**Robert M. Baumbach** has been an art teacher at State College Area High School for twenty years. Fifteen years ago, he instituted the school's photography curriculum.
*"For some time I had an image in mind of the school buses and traffic between the two high school campuses in the early morning sunshine. I see it often on my way to work. This project gave me a reason to finally try this image. It was a great day, though I was hoping for more atmospheric effect with puffy exhaust in the cold air."*

**John Bellanti** is a psychologist with Psychological Associates of Central Pennsylvania who *"helps people to work for*

wholeness in their lives."
*"My family and I came to State College in 1964 for one year so that I could attend graduate school at Penn State. We are still here all these years later! We fell in love with the picturesqueness of this town. I've taken many images of State College over those years, and I thought this project was a good excuse to take some more. For me, photography is up close and intimate — attempting to capture the essence of the person."*

**Adam Bergeman** is now in first grade at Lemont Elementary School. When he participated in this project as a kindergarten student, he explained:
*"I like to take pictures of stuff so that I can see what they look like and I can remember them. I'm a kid. I like to saw and hammer at the workbench at school. I like to read a lot!"*

**Arthur Beward** is a retired associate professor of photographic science at the Rochester Institute of Technology. Despite a full-time career at R.I.T. in New York, he has kept a permanent residence in State College for fifty-

seven years. He considers himself an almost lifelong resident.
*"I've seen the town change since I was a Penn State student here studying chemistry. State College is a growing town. It is not a rural village any longer."*

**David Beyerle** is a communications engineer in the Office of Telecommunications at Penn State.
*"I did not have an 'assignment' per se. I simply embarked on foot with camera and tripod in hand, accompanied by my wife, Susan, along with our two-month-old daughter, Laura. We began at our home at the corner of South Gill Street and West Nittany Avenue, headed to Holmes-Foster Park, and then toward downtown. After I had photographed two workmen at the rear of the Chili's construction site on South Allen Street, one of them remarked that I was the twelfth person to have photographed them that day!"*

**Stacie Bird** is a photographer and digital imaging specialist with the College of Agricultural Sciences at Penn State.
*"I chose to photograph people*

and things I'm familiar with — that make me feel something. I live next door to a farm owned by the Homan family just outside of State College, and I made it a priority to photograph them. I've lived in State College for a long time, and I've seen our agricultural resources shrink remarkably. My house is surrounded by cornfields. I want to make sure that people in the future know that we were once encircled by farms."*

**Arthur Boller** is a Penn State student who participated on assignment for a photojournalism class.
*"I was wandering around campus searching for picture possibilities when I spotted a student on roller blades doing stunts on the steps of Willard Building. I wanted to get a dramatic shot of his 'jumping' the steps, so I waited at the bottom of the steps for him to leap. There wasn't much room for him to land where I was and he nearly jumped onto me! I couldn't resist calling this image 'Leap of Faith.'"*

**Matthew F. Brashears** is a Penn State student and photographer for *The Daily*

*Collegian* who participated in this project for a photojournalism class.

"On campus in the evening, I spotted three women on their way to a sorority rush party. Obviously their heels weren't very comfortable because they stopped to adjust them several times and needed each other's support for balance. It just amused me — so I shot it."

**Lois R. Chavern** is a microbiologist who spent much of her life working in public health. She recently retired from Penn State, where she taught microbiology at the McKeesport Campus. She first spent time in State College while pursuing her undergraduate degree at Penn State and enjoyed this area so much that she returned when she retired.

"For this project I decided to document the activities of the 'seniors' — my peer group. Most interesting is the vitality of many of our seniors who live with zest and good spirits. Many contribute to this community by volunteering. I photograph older people, in part, to show them enjoying themselves while participating in a wide variety of activities. That was my photographic objective for the Centennial."

**Li Chen** is a Penn State graduate who was working at The Film Center in September 1994. She now lives in New York City where she works for a stock photography agency while establishing herself as a specialist in dance and theater photography.

"On September 12, 1994, I had to juggle shooting for the Centennial in between my work schedule. Though it was hectic, I was eager to participate in such an exciting and important event. I tried to cover as much territory as possible. As I was photographing the birds on the wire downtown, I was thinking about the Alfred Hitchcock movie 'The Birds.' In the fall, these flocks of birds seem to be as much a part of the town as the people."

**Alice E. Clark** is executive director of Heritage I. She has a degree from Penn State in art history, with an emphasis in photographic history.

"I worked at my job from 7:30 am to 10:30 pm on September 12, 1994, and still managed to take five-plus rolls of film. I photographed everywhere I went that day, even on my way to and from various appointments. I participated in this project because of my interest

in photojournalism and to give something back to a community that has been very enjoyable for my husband and me."

**James Collins** is a freelance graphic designer and photographer. Originally from the Boston area, he has lived in State College since 1980. He is enthusiastic about exploring varied areas of interest ranging from electrically controlled model aircraft to philosophy.

"After graduating from college, I couldn't think of any place I'd rather live than in a college town, and State College pretty well defines that description. Unfit for normal employment, I take pictures and create graphic design, which I like doing very much. I hope our son Dan and his friends will enjoy seeing the picture of themselves as well as the other pictures in this book in later years."

**Anne Quinn Corr** is a freelance writer, caterer, and former owner of Q's Café at Encore Books & Espresso.

"I participated because of my interest in chronicling a specific moment in time for the historical record."

**Richard L. Crowley** is a retired purchasing officer for Penn State, for whom photography has been a serious avocation for fifty years. His work has appeared in numerous publications. He has been an officer for photography groups, local as well as national, and he teaches photography.

"I've been taking pictures around here for twenty-five years. I really thought at great length of what I should photograph. What would future residents find interesting? I was trying to 'make' the pictures rather than just take them. As a Penn State staffer at the time, I chose the campus as my image territory and made arrangements to photograph in special places like Old Main. I photographed the Penn State smokestack to depict energy use at this point in time because technology changes so quickly. Who knows what the world will look like in 100 years!"

**Maryann Curione** is a photojournalist who specializes in photographing people at their workplaces. She is building a body of work (in photographs and oral histories) about the small businesses of Centre

County, which she exhibits periodically and which she hopes to build into a book.

"It is the descriptive quality of photographs that intrigues me most. The minutiae in photographs (clothing, architecture, signage) are clues to the culture of an era. I use the camera primarily as an anthropologic tool to describe visual details. I prefer using a view camera because of its versatility and fine image resolving powers. For the Centennial, I assigned myself the task of photographing State College police officers, firefighters, and ambulance crews because I wanted to meet the people whose job it is to keep us safe and to honor them by including them in this book."

**Ronald A. Davis** is assistant borough manager for State College. He has worked for the borough for twenty-five years — one-quarter of the borough's existence.

"I photographed in the downtown purposefully to document the many inviting niches that have been designed with pedestrians in mind: niches that include public artworks, benches, and landscaped areas. Traditionally, the community has been committed to preserving the charm of its neighborhoods and the downtown business district."

**Marion R. Deppen** is retired from the College of Agricultural Sciences at Penn State. He now operates a mountain tree farm called "Deppen Woodlands." He has had several photographs published as magazine covers for *Pennsylvania Forests.*

*"Photography has taught me how 'to see' and appreciate so much more of the world. Color photography allows you to make more vibrant what real life is like. Through photography, you can record and enhance the absolute best version of an image for posterity."*

**James R. DeTuerk** is an associate professor of landscape architecture at Penn State.

*"As a photographer, I am interested in how people use their outdoor environment."*

**John Dickison** is a videographer with the College of Agricultural Sciences at Penn State. His dog, Cosmo, is a local celebrity and columnist for the newspaper *Voices of Central Pennsylvania.* Cosmo dispenses words of wisdom on any topic imaginable, from Elvis sightings to advice to the lovelorn.

*"My friend and colleague, Steve Williams, recruited me for this project. Among other things, I wanted to document how we do our banking—at the walk-up/drive-up MAC machines. Perhaps in the future we will be banking by telephone or television."*

**Kim Dionis** is a writer who lives in Boalsburg.

*"This area has changed a lot since I moved here in the summer of '80. Someday—in the not so distant future—much of what we photograph today will be gone. This book will show me where I've been."*

**Richard H. Dixon, M.D.**, is an oncologist with Internal Medicine Associates of State College.

*"I photograph to capture the intimacy of common life experiences and to capture fleeting moments in time. For this project, I assigned myself the job of portraying the night shift at Centre Community Hospital—a critical but often unrecognized aspect of patient care. I wanted to show the 'human' side of the hospital late at night."*

**Marian Cannon Dornell** is a retired registered nurse who specialized in psychiatric, mental health, and hospice nursing. She credits these experiences of sharing potent moments in people's lives with making her a careful observer and informing her photography.

*"Although my father was a professional photographer, I was content taking a nice snapshot of family and social events until my husband gave me a 'serious' camera as a gift recently. In this brief time, I've become caught up in the art and science of photography, grabbing every opportunity to capture a color, mood, or moment."*

**Scott Elmquist** is a writer/ photographer for the Penn State Alumni Association. He also freelances for the *Centre Daily Times, Town & Gown* magazine, Studio 2 Photography, and The Smeal College of Business at Penn State.

*"The shoot really opened my eyes to the photographic possibilities of the area. I tried to stay out of downtown, and instead, worked the periphery of State College. I saw only a couple of other photographers and met some great people. Most of my photos were spur of the moment, taking less than five minutes to shoot. The whole day turned out to be great fun!"*

**Robert L. Fantauzzo** is President of InSyst, a local computer consulting firm specializing in data base applications and data analysis.

*"I grew up in the shadows of Kodak Park and started taking pictures with a Kodak Brownie when I was eight years old. I have had a great interest in photography ever since and have run through almost as many cameras as I have rolls of film. For this project I attempted to capture my perception of State College's sense of place. Previously, I worked in Washington, D.C., and when I married, I moved here. I've been here now for eleven years. I like to call this my 'new' home. For me, it's a mix of small-town civility mixed with the vibrancy of the big city."*

**Ralph Fearing** is a retired industrial chemist.

*"I spent my day photographing well-known people, activities, and institutions in State College."*

**Kim N. Fisher** is the humanities reference librarian at Penn State's Pattee Library. He has exhibited his photographs locally.

*"I like to capture the serenity of nature or to strike some mood in my work. I participated because I knew it would be a challenge and fun."*

**Charles A. Fitzgerald** is pastor for the Wesley United Methodist Church in Tyrone, Pa. For twenty-three years, he has been a freelance photographer for newspapers and other publications.

*"I see photographs as an expression of one's personality and experience in life. My photography has changed in content and style as I have grown older. This was a very emotional day for me, as I was reminiscing while photographing. I desired to capture childhood memories—to remember and share my early life in State College."*

**John C. Flohr** is president of Consultation and Development Group, a company that provides, among other things, management and computer systems consultation and development.

*"As area residents and*

photographers, my son, Scott, and I were delighted to contribute to the community and indulge in our passion for photography. We both have busy schedules. We look for opportunities to do things together. We traveled together throughout that day. We began shooting at dawn while Scott was working his paper route and wrapped up at night. It was a great day shooting with my son. Thanks for the opportunity!"

**Scott Flohr** is a senior at State College Area High School, where he has appeared on stage in many roles as a State High Thespian. In the summers, he works backstage and performs on stage with the State College Community Theatre at the Boal Barn Playhouse.

*"I have been influenced mostly by my father, who introduced photography to me at an early age. My dad and I have taken several excursions abroad to photograph in Europe. But I rarely get the chance to take photographs here at home. We approached this project as a team. Before the shoot day, we shared ideas and decided upon an itinerary. We photographed nearly the whole day, coming home in the afternoon to rest and regroup before heading out*

again for the evening. It was a lot of fun, especially to do it with my father, because I really respect and admire him."

**Rita Foderaro** was the first president of the Holmes-Foster Neighborhood Association and lives in one of the borough's historic stone homes. She was also a member of the State College Borough Planning Commission. She is now active with the Pennsylvania Prison Society, an advocacy agency for prisoners.

*"I've lived here since 1960. I love it here! State College has vital neighborhoods. It was a wonderful place to raise children. I hope that we are still a residential community 100 years from now."*

**Drew C. Frank** sells construction tools and supplies to the construction industry in the Centre Region. He also operates Meadow Lane Photography, which specializes in portraits, weddings, and commercial photography.

*"When I arrived at The Diner with my camera at 5:45 am and found that I was scooped by someone crazier than I am, I knew then that it was going to be a long day! Fourteen hours later, at 8 pm, I drove up*

to Pine Grove Mountain to catch the sunset, only to find two of my fellow photographers already there! Thank you for letting me be a part of this great event."

**Rod Fye** is the produce manager at Bi Lo Supermarket.

*"At 6 am, while I was photographing downtown, I spotted a fellow photographer walking down the street shaking his head repeating the phrase, 'I must be crazy. I must be crazy!'"*

**Jennifer Garringer** graduated from Penn State in May 1995, with a bachelor of fine arts degree, with a concentration in photography and an art history minor. She was a photographer for *The Daily Collegian.*

*"My reason for participating in this project was to get as much photographic experience as I could. My attitude is, 'just go for it!' I like the control of photography. I don't believe you take a picture; you compose it. I know when I shoot, before the film is even developed, which photos I'll want to print. I am attracted to chaotic places because I like to find the order in visual chaos."*

**Matthew L. Garrity** is a Penn State student who participated on assignment for a graphic design class.

*"Penn State and State College are intertwined in many ways. Fraternity houses have long been a part of both the campus and the town. I chose to photograph fraternity life because historically, it has been a memorable part of the collegiate experience for many Penn Staters."*

**Clarissa I. González** is a Penn State student and a photographer for *The Daily Collegian.*

*"Basically, all of my shots were taken as I was walking to and from my classes. I wanted to record the State College I see every day. I was especially conscious of photographing the bits of beauty in the downtown: like window boxes filled with flowers, cute storefronts, and interesting doorways."*

**Mary Sue Henszey** has been taking photographs for twenty-five years and has worked as a freelance photographer for clients such as *Sailing Magazine* and Dartmouth College. She has also taught photography for elderhostels.

*"As a nature lover, I was drawn to photographing in*

places that would highlight the richness of the natural resources in our area, like rolling farmland and the birds at Shaver's Creek Environmental Center."

**Brian Hill**, born and raised in State College, is now a financial planner living in Pittsburgh. In September 1994, he was working part-time for The Film Center while attending graduate school at Penn State.

*"My family still lives here. We are all Penn State alums and huge Nittany Lion fans. I really like Happy Valley. I'd like to be able to come back to State College to work and live. I participated in order to share my love for State College through my photographs. While I was shooting, I encountered twelve other photographers. We would share stories about our adventures so far and then head out in different directions to continue shooting."*

**Michael T. Jesky** is a Penn State graduate with a degree in photojournalism. He is now a reporter for the *Hazleton Standard-Speaker.*

*"Because of my class schedule on that day, I could devote only one hour to this project. I like to remain unobtrusive as a*

photographer and record what I observe around me. With only one hour available, I was getting worried that I wouldn't encounter anything particularly interesting. But in my last five minutes, I came upon a student sprawled along a wall studying and knew I had finally found my subject!"

**Clarence D. Johnson, Jr.,** is a twenty-four-year veteran police officer with Penn State who is called upon on occasion to photograph crime scenes.
"I wanted to be a photographer for this project out of my appreciation for State College and Penn State, which provide the benefits of a larger city in a rural setting. Trying to photograph as much as possible on September 12, I made some photographs while in my police uniform."

**Denny Kaltreider** teaches visual arts at the State College Area Junior High School and also teaches photo courses for teachers. He was a Vietnam combat photographer. His photographic work is made available through Visuals Unlimited, a stock photography agency in New Hampshire which represents him.

"I have been very much influenced by the work of Ansel Adams and Roger Tory Peterson. Nature continually reveals its innermost secrets to us through photography and serene meditation."

**Barbara J. Kasales** is a custom picture framer.
"The weather was perfect. It was fun to see things I see everyday but with a critical eye. We were permitted to photograph on the outskirts of State College, so I decided to photograph my village of Lemont. State College is still rather small and is surrounded by some even smaller communities. This is part of what makes this region feel cozy."

**Norma Keller** is Director of the Centre County Youth Service Bureau. She also operates Pathway Photos, through which she sells her travel and underwater photography.
"I raised my son in this community, and this project was a way for me to recapture moments that were meaningful in his life. I chose 'children' as my subject because I wanted to acknowledge that there is a significant need in this community for human services and to show that there are many people and agencies

working in the trenches trying to meet that need."

**Sue P. LaBrecque** is a homemaker and a community volunteer. She works part-time for the State College Area School District.
"I've been here since I graduated from Penn State in 1979, and then stayed on to get my master's degree. I wanted to participate in this project because I love this town so much. This is a great place for families to raise children. Here, neighbors care for each other and look after each other's children."

**Jock Lauterer** is an assistant professor of journalism at Penn State. For fifteen years, he ran his own small-town newspaper in the South. He is the author of several books, including *Hog Wild: A Back-to-the-Land Saga*, a memoir of his experiences on his farmstead in the Appalachians. On September 12, 1994, he assigned his photojournalism students to photograph State College and its environs as part of this Centennial project and their course work.
"I didn't really plan the shot of my students all peering up at

me with their cameras until early that morning when I realized that I needed to see for myself that these fledgling shooters knew how to hold their cameras and focus properly—this being their first assignment! While I was briefing them from the steps of Carnegie Building, I knew immediately and instinctively that I had to make that photograph."

**Edward Leos** came to Penn State in 1946 to head the new still-photography unit. In 1962, he became a full-time faculty member of the School of Journalism, where he taught photojournalism until 1978, when he retired. He is the author of the book *Other Summers: The Photographs of Horace Engle*, which features the 'concealed vest' camera images of a Victorian photographer.
"I thought this project was a good outlet for a community to express itself. I was intrigued by the possibility of marshaling hordes of camera users—citizens—people—and gathering glimpses of what life here at this particular time is like."

**Marc B. Levey** works for the Office of the Vice Provost for Educational

Equity at Penn State, where he produces, among other things, educational videos on diversity. He and his business partner, I. Jeanne Miller, own and operate Visual Design Associates, through which they create images for state, national, and international tourism authorities. He is the author of books on photography, including *The Art of Autofocus Photography*.
"Photographers were falling all over each other downtown on September 12. We had to make an arrangement to get out of each other's way since many of us were shooting in the same spaces. And, yet the marvelous thing is that all of our images were different. It was as if we were each photographing on different planets! I believe that all images are singular experiences and are autobiographical."

**Karen Lintner** is an art teacher at the State College Area Junior High School.
"I had very little time to shoot, as I did not leave school until 4 pm, so I went to a few spots I had in mind. Everywhere I went I saw photographers! As an art teacher, I am sensitive to color and composition. I am always looking. During the

shoot, I found myself captivated by the luminous quality of the day. It was a brilliant, clear day with a deep blue sky that made for saturated colors and dramatic reflections."

**Pat Little** has been photographing for the *Centre Daily Times* for thirteen years and is the chief photographer there. "This is my hometown. I was born in Bellefonte and raised in State College. It's interesting to see the physical changes in this area. But the essence of the town never changes. It's still a student town — the median age is twenty. That's the way it always was. That's the way it always will be. That's good! The youthful energy of the college students is invigorating. As a photojournalist, my motto is: 'Be there and be ready for anything!'"

**Kathy D. Long** graduated from Penn State in January 1994, with a degree in arts and architecture and an emphasis in photography. "I love to take photographs outside, especially while taking walks in the woods or mountains. I believe that's how I came to take the picture of the Nittany Lion shrine. I wanted a different and a new

view of the lion shrine — something that I hadn't seen done before."

**Peter S. Marshall** has served as borough manager for State College since 1986. "Daily life in State College is a fantastic dance of thousands of complex human beings, all unique and yet all connected to one another. One of the many borough employees whom I photographed on this day was Dick Waltz, a foreman in the State College Public Works Department. His work, his thoughts, his emotions have added to the wonderful rhythm of this community for almost forty years. I am honored to be able to reveal, through my photography, one of the many special, but often unrecognized, people who contribute to the community mightily day in and day out, season after season. I am proud of our local government. I am proud of those who labor to advance its cause. I am proud to be part of the dance."

**Helena Lukas Martemucci** is pursuing a master of fine arts degree at Penn State. "Photography has been a part of my life since childhood because that was my father's passion and profession. Visual

expression is easier for me than verbal and that is part of my attraction to photography. Dancing has always been important to me, so it was natural for me to choose it as my assignment for September 12, 1994."

**Tonya Lynn Martin** graduated from State High and earned a bachelor of arts degree in advertising at Penn State. She worked for the *Centre Daily Times* as an advertising account manager for five years. She is now taking photography courses with the expectation of a career in photography. "I have lived in State College all but four years of my life. As a native, I probably have a different perspective. Penn State is a big influence on State College, but it does not define it. State College has a personality all its own. I have fond memories of growing up here — of spending time in special places, some of which, unfortunately, no longer exist. For this project, I spent twelve hours photographing the people that are dear to me and places that make State College unique — like Meyer Dairy. I also wanted to capture the natural beauty of this area's landscape and animals."

**Jay C. Mastalerz** is manager of CPI Photo Finish at the Nittany Mall. A professional photographer for thirteen years, he operates Keystone Photographic Service, which has him traveling all over the Mid-Atlantic States as a wedding photographer. "I was born and raised here. For this project, I decided to revisit places where once I spent a lot of time: the high school and Community Field. It was a trip down memory lane. My assignment was 'leisure activity and sports,' so I drove around to find athletic activities. Luckily, I happened upon the Little Lions football game, which led me to the tennis courts, which led me to the softball fields. The more I looked, the more I found."

**Heather McDermott** recently graduated from Penn State with a journalism degree. For this project she assigned herself the task of photographing the morning rituals of residents, which included finding the breakfast regulars at downtown restaurants. "I shoot only what pleases me aesthetically. Simply stated, if I like it, I shoot it."

**Stephen McGregor** is program director at Penn State's Industrial Research Office, where he develops mutually beneficial relationships between the university and industry. "I learned about this project the morning of September 12, on the radio. I'm just happy that I had a few rolls of film available so that I could participate on short notice. I am notorious in my family for taking pictures of them, so it came as little surprise that I would make them my photographic subjects for this day. I liked the concept of this project and thought that the book would serve as a composite snapshot of the community. Altogether, we photographers captured one moment in the history of State College. I was proud to be part of this effort."

**Annette Shirey McHugh** has been a full-time community volunteer for much of her life and has served as "official" photographer for various civic organizations. She is a member of the State College Woman's Club and the Art Alliance of Central Pennsylvania. "For this project I decided to photograph the architecture of area houses of worship. After spending several hours photographing churches, I was driving up College Avenue and just two cars in front of me there was a van with a sign: 'Have you Been to Church Lately?'"

**Pamela A. McHugh** sells software for Minitab, a statistical software company that sells its products worldwide.
"I first learned about this project upon returning from a month of driving around out West searching for a new place to settle down. Once home, I realized that the most enchanting place I encountered was my hometown, State College. Although I have no formal photographic training, being involved in this project was thrilling for me because the idea of freezing moments in time for future State Collegians to appreciate was the perfect way to celebrate my decision to remain a permanent 'fixture' of Happy Valley. There is a bittersweetness to life here, though—since your friends and neighbors seem to come and go with each semester. The sweetness comes with getting to know people of vastly different backgrounds who bring a freshness to your life and to the town. However, it's always in the back of your mind that they'll be leaving

when their time at the university is finished—that's the difficult part of living in a college town."

**Russell V. Meyers** is a Staff Engineer at HRB Systems. He is president of the Mount Nittany Chapter of the American Wine Society, which explains why he chose to document the activities at area wineries.
"I believe that Pennsylvania wine is under-appreciated. Our local wineries produce award-wining varietals. I wanted to help advance the wine industry in the Centre Region by having it depicted for this Centennial collection. The day before the shoot, I met with the owners of several wineries and explained the project to them. Of course, they were happy to participate. I spent the day photographing various aspects of wine making — from grape growing to bottling. I thoroughly enjoyed myself while undertaking the assignment."

**I. Jeanne Miller** is a photographer and partner (with Marc B. Levey) in Visual Design Associates. Among their clients are the states of Florida and New Mexico, and the municipalities of San Francisco, Montreal, and Quebec

City. When they are not photographing for themselves or for clients, they teach photography and conduct outdoor workshops on photographing wildlife.
"Photography started for me as an avocation but it has turned into a profession. Being a Penn State alumna and now a State College resident, I feel an affinity for this town—a closeness that spans many years. It was a joy to look for the daily goings-on in State College on that special Monday."

**Chuck Mong** is president of the Chamber of Business and Industry of Centre County. He is perhaps equally well known to area residents for his performances as a member of the Nittany Knights, a forty-member barbershop chorus.
"Given the nature of my work in this community, I decided to photograph the business leaders of this area. I concentrated particularly on portraying multi-generational, family businesses, because they are an important part of our local economy and our town history. My subjects kindly adjusted their schedules so that I could make a portrait of them at their businesses. It

was one of my most exciting days in Centre County."

**Erman M. Moon** is a construction superintendent for the Bryce Jordan Center building project at Penn State.
"My work at the Bryce Jordan Center gave me a perfect opportunity to photograph the construction site from the inside. I knew that it would make a good subject because so many different work activities are going on simultaneously. There is a great variety of picture possibilities. Because of the nature of my work, my family and I have lived in various parts of the country. We know that once the Jordan Center is completed and we leave here that we will take with us memories of the hospitality we were shown by this community."

**Eugene W. Moon** is a carpenter for the Bryce Jordan Center building project at Penn State.
"My dad and I are proud of our work and wanted to participate so that we could show what is involved in a construction project of this magnitude. We wanted to show not only the interesting shapes of the interior structures being built, but also the people who erect them."

**Suzanne H. Motley** is a welder for New Holland in Belleville, manufacturers of farm equipment.
"I am a spur-of-the-moment photographer. I keep a loaded camera in my car so that I can jump out when something strikes me. I like to photograph people and animals in action, on the move. I like the look of speed in my images—things in the midst of happening."

**Julie L. Nash** is a Penn State student studying journalism and political science. Her philosophy about photography is:
"Shoot and hope for something!"

**Donna M. Neufer** is a Customer Service Associate at Lowe's Home Improvement Center.
"While growing up I have always had some type of camera. I attempt to keep a running history in pictures of my family and friends and of spectacular events and scenery."

**Howard P. Nuernberger** has more than twenty years' experience as a professional photographer. Currently, he works as a photographer for Agricultural Information Services in the College of Agricultural Sciences, Penn State. *"I chose for my assignment, University Park Airport because I wanted to photograph something I knew about. Also, current aircraft are 'state of the art' for only a short time and therefore an excellent reference for their era. Airport manager Bob Dannaker and his employees made the assignment easy for me."*

**Richard S. Orr** is a senior industrial photographer at HRB Systems. He first worked at HRB as a darkroom technician for twenty years, then as an industrial photographer there for fourteen years. *"I thought the public might like to see what goes on here at HRB. It is an interesting workplace that makes for compelling images. My co-workers were very cooperative about being photographed for this historical project. I wanted to capture people working at their usual tasks, thereby showing their skills with various types of technology."*

**Raegan Owens** works as a counselor for the Community Foundation for Human Development, which provides residential living for mentally handicapped adults in Bethlehem, Pa.

*"I'm just addicted to my camera. I found out about the project when, as I was walking downtown one day with a camera strapped around me, someone stopped me and asked me if I wanted to participate. I chose as my subjects the senior citizens center and the Association for Retarded Citizens, because I wanted to be sure that these social service agencies would be represented as part of the community for this book."*

**Linda J. Pagani** is senior merchandise manager for J.C. Penney in State College.
*"I photographed my husband, Wayne Pagani, owner of Arby's, and my son, David, as they were practicing archery in our backyard. Wayne taught our son, as a youngster, how to use a bow and arrow. Wayne believes that you should take your son hunting instead of hunting for your son — meaning that shared activities make for a strong and loving family."*

**David S. Palermo** is retired from the Department of Psychology at Penn State.
*"I now devote a major portion of my time to taking courses in photography, taking photographs, and showing my*

*work in exhibits and arts festivals. I have not settled on any single theme in my work, although I feel that there is a thread of romanticism in what I do. People were extraordinarily cooperative when I photographed them on September 12. There were some initial suspicions about the reasons for my taking pictures, but once I was able to show my Centennial press badge and explain the project, everyone wanted to participate."*

**Philip I. Park** is president and CEO of Local Government Research Corporation, a management consulting firm based in State College. A longterm area resident, he served in local government as a supervisor for Patton Township from 1978 to 1995.
*"The greatest challenge is to find a worthwhile photograph in what we see every day. I found this project required a lot of mental energy to concentrate on finding photographic possibilities. I discovered that, at least at sunrise, we enthusiastic amateurs were as thick as fleas. The challenge was fun. However, I do not think I will quit my day job."*

**Elizabeth H. Pennock** is a music teacher for grades

K-6 in the Penns Valley Area School District. Her photographs have won several awards.
*"It's my husband, Roger's, fault that I am a photographer. For many years, when we vacationed, he would take many, many pictures. Invariably, I was always waiting for him to 'take just one more shot.' At first I complained that he spent too much of our traveling time photographing. But soon, I got hooked on photography and joined forces with him. In fact, now when planning our vacations, we think: 'Where can we go to get good pictures?' For this project, I wanted to photograph the lovely stores downtown where I do most of my shopping. I enjoy strolling along College Avenue."*

**Roger Pennock, Jr.**, is a retired professor of agronomy at Penn State, where he was honored as the first recipient of "The Award for Excellence in Teaching." He also has won local and national awards for his photography.
*"I started in photography in 1946 with a 35 mm camera that my father bought for $6.50 at a fire sale. My wife, Libby, and I heard about this Centennial photography*

*project and thought it would be nice to get something in a local publication that would be long-lived. We wanted to be part of something that had far-reaching historical importance."*

**Michele Polignone** graduated from Penn State in May 1995, with a bachelor of arts in broadcast journalism with an emphasis on photojournalism. She now works as a videographer for television station WWCP/WATM in Altoona/Johnstown. She also teaches photography at the Hetzel Union Center for Arts and Crafts at Penn State.
*"This photograph of Sammy was the very first photograph I ever took on assignment as a photojournalist. It is unbelievable that my first image ever made it into this book. I know it's due to Sammy, the young boy with a toy pistol who tried to arrest Penn State students on their way to the library. He was a terrific subject!"*

**Robert J. Price** is Executive Director of Downtown State College, an organization committed to fostering the economic health of the downtown.

*"When I signed up for this project, I immediately knew what I should photograph: the clusters of children I see around town every day walking or riding in strollers with their care takers. I prepared for the shoot by buying a panoramic camera so that I could fit as many children into each frame as possible. On September 12, I left my office and set out to search for them and found several groups of them along College Avenue. The kids themselves were real 'hams.' The international flavor of what I call the 'Toddler Parade' has become part of the downtown landscape itself. I wanted to document this delightful sight because it brings smiles to our faces."*

**H. A. Rader** is a retired electronics technician for Penn State. He now operates his own business, specializing in photography, videography, and audio visual productions. For many years, he designed the equipment set up for the International Slide Salon for the Central Pennsylvania Festival of the Arts.

*"My assignments were 'night photography', 'people at their jobs', and 'Asian stores and restaurants'. I started taking pictures at midnight along fraternity row. From there, I cruised downtown in my car, hunting for pictures. I'm kind of a night owl anyway, so I enjoyed roaming the town in the dark. I felt a responsibility to complete my assignments as best I could, so I spent nearly the whole day shooting except for five hours in the afternoon when I caught some sleep. I wanted to participate because I've lived in this community since the 1960s. I met my wife here, and I've developed many dear friendships here. My ties to State College go back even further because my father was a Penn State graduate of the class of 1909."*

**Nova Ritchey** is a senior at State High. She plans to pursue her love of photography in college and, perhaps, to make of it a career.

*"My teacher, Bob Baumbach, assigned our Photography II class to photograph around the school and said that the best images would be submitted to the Centennial. I took the hallway picture because I liked the perspective. My dad, who teaches art at the high school, and my uncle, who was a professional photographer for a while, have instilled in me an appreciation for photographic images. For my personal photography, I take a lot of pictures of my dog, á la the whimsical Weimaraner dog portraits of William Wegman."*

**Paul D. Ruby** works for Murata Electronics and is a fine-arts photographer who has used a view camera for his photographs since 1980. Paul has attended many fine-arts photography workshops, including Ansel Adams and Paul Caponigro. In fact, he returned from the Caponigro workshop just in time for the photo essay project.

*"While the group portait of the centennial photographers was being set up for the Centre Daily Times, my seven-year-old daughter, Allison, showed me her second-grade class teddy bear. It was her turn to take it home for the weekend and to write down the adventures Buddy had. We agreed that I should hold Buddy in the group photo. So Buddy got his picture on the front page of the newspaper. When Allison's teacher, Mrs. Davis (St. John's School, Bellefonte), read Allison's essay and saw the newspaper, she sent a note home with Allison requesting that I complete my own essay about Buddy's adventure. My essay and Buddy's newspaper photograph with the photographers are included in a book with the students' essays."*

**Cathy Seith** is a staff photographer for the *Durham Herald-Sun* in Durham, N. C. At the time she participated in this project, she was a staff photographer for the *Centre Daily Times*. While she was still living in State College, Cathy and her photojournalism were the subject of a feature about the Missouri Photographic Workshop broadcast by the ABC news magazine, "Prime-Time Live."

*"In September 1994, I had been living and working in State College for exactly one year. As a CDT photographer, I thought I could find some interesting nooks and crannies that other people might overlook. I photographed nearly all day. I was exhausted at the end, but it was an exhilarating experience. I learned a lot from being a photo editor for this project. I saw what images we got, what we missed, and how I would approach this type of project in the future, as both a photographer and an editor."*

**Mark Selders** is store manager for The Film Center. He also works as a freelance photographer specializing in sports photography. Appropriately, he sent himself to Penn State to photograph JoePa and the Nittany Lions on the practice field, where he "tried to capture the action at its peak, reflecting the emotion of the moment."

*"While shooting on this day, I encountered photographers everywhere! As I pulled into the Joe Hays Overlook at the top of Pine Grove Mountain, there was already someone there. I set up; he tore down. About twenty minutes later, another photographer arrived. We proceeded to talk about the day while watching the darkness fall over State College. Twenty minutes later, still another photographer arrived. He photographed us as we photographed the valley below. We all chatted for a while then moved on to other locales."*

**Stephanie Seraydarian** recently graduated from Penn State with a major in international politics and a minor in Spanish. In December 1994, she photographed in the rebel territory of Chiapas, Mexico, during the Zapatista rebel uprising. Her long-term goal is to publish a book of photos and text about the socio-economic state of Latin America. She wants to use photography as a social tool to document what she calls "undeniable reality."

*"I want to use photography for political purposes—among them, to portray disappearing cultures and to show social ills that need correcting. Images that are powerful can covince people about the existence and urgency of a problem. As the adage goes, 'seeing is believing.'"*

**Ellen M. Sherwood** has lived in this area for twenty-four years. She has been an active volunteer for community projects and is currently vice-president of the Lemont Women's Club.

*"Because my husband is a pilot, I thought I'd take aerial pictures. I didn't think anyone else would. I wanted to be different. Once we were in the air, I realized that I only had a half a roll of film left in my camera, so I knew that I couldn't waste any negatives. I had to be extremely careful to frame each image as well as possible while taking into account the position and movement of the plane. I love this area and especially Mt. Nittany, which we see from our home and which we climb often. I wanted to show how lovely the land is here."*

**Alan John Sidwar** is a residential counselor at Strawberry Fields, an agency providing opportunities for personal growth and independence for persons with disabilities.

*"I found out about this photo project at the last minute, by accident, when I went to the Camera Shop to buy film. I only had time to photograph during my lunch hour, so I concentrated on photographing downtown near where I live. My mailman, Carmine Dinello, is well known, and I thought he would make a good subject. I walk around downtown each day and always find something or someone new and special to appreciate. The town and campus are beautiful."*

**Mark Smeal** teaches third grade at Houserville Elementary School.

*"To participate in this Centennial project, each classroom in our school received a camera with film to take pictures of class activities throughout the day. I photographed my students as they went about their usual tasks: sitting in their desks, writing at the blackboard, packing up their books at the end of the day."*

**Carolyn Clinefelter Smith**, a State College resident for most of her life, serves on many local "ABCs" (authorities, boards, and commissions). She is a member of the Centre County Historical Society and the State College Centennial Commission. For the Centennial celebration, she is curating a year-long series of exhibits of historic State College photographs, many of which, at more than a century old, tell as much about the history of photography as they do about the history of State College.

*"Because of my work with the historic photographs of the State College Centennial Collection, which reflect our past, I know how important it is to document our present. From studying old photographs, I realize what we need to record for the future. That's why this project, which involves documenting State College as we experience it today, is so significant. By preserving the present pictorially we contribute to the historic record of our town. And that's why I will continue to photograph State College until I die."*

**Eric Smith** is a third grader at Houserville Elementary School. When he photographed for this project, he was seven years old and a student in Judy Strayer's second-grade class at Lemont Elementary School. During school vacations, he accompanies his dad (who drives moving vans for Hoy Transfer) on trips across the country, visiting Texas, Montana, Idaho, Washington and many other states. His mom, Janice, says: "He is an all-around great kid! He loves baseball and playing with his neighborhood friends. In school, he likes math. He's a hard worker who even likes to help out with chores at home."

**Mary Lou Snitger** is retired from Penn State, where she worked as a photographer for seventeen years.

*"I was born into photography. My father was a photographer, and I helped him in his studio. Photography to me is a 'happy' pursuit. I derive a lot of pleasure from composing images. I wanted to participate because I've been a long-term resident of this area—for forty-five-plus years. I wanted to become part of the*

*Centennial and thought my best way was using what I know—photography. It was inspiring seeing and talking to other photographers along the way that day."*

**Kristin Breslin Sommese** is an assistant professor of Graphic Design at the School of Visual Arts at Penn State, where she teaches graphic design and photo/design. She assigned her students to photograph State College for this Centennial event as part of a course on photo/design.

*"As a fine-arts photographer, I have been more interested in controlled studio situations than in candid photography. I try to create a fantasy through the use of lighting, costume, and subject matter."*

**Lanny Sommese** is a professor of art at the School of Visual Arts at Penn State. He has won international awards for his graphic designs and is known locally for the posters he has created for the Central Pennsylvania Festival of the Arts.

*"In my photography, I attempt to fuse a juxtaposition of form and content at a particular instant to make a statement that goes beyond subject matter and the moment. I decided to*

make photographs of playground equipment near my house in College Heights. While I was shooting, a mother brought her young kids over to the playground. They kept getting on my bouncy subjects."

**Judy Strayer** is a teacher at Lemont Elementary School. On the photo registration form that accompanied the packet of photographs of her class, she wrote under 'occupation': "I teach these beautiful children!"
*"I just love the natural beauty that children possess — that is easily captured in photography. Monday, September 12, 1994, was a typical happy day at the school playground. In our class, we have many special times when we do things as a group. We especially enjoy singing altogether. This photo was taken at the end of an activity when we wondered if we could all fit on the climber in the playground. We did!"*

**Lois Todd** teaches basic reading and math skills to disabled adults at the Development Center for Adults.
*"I try to look for beauty in ordinary scenes and objects that we see and sometimes overlook every day. Everyone*

who caught me photographing them wanted to 'pose' and everyone said, 'What's this for? Am I going to be in the paper?'"

**Steve Tressler** is a photographer with University Photo/Graphics at Penn State. Recently, he has been concentrating on producing a series of black and white portrait photographs of people of notoriety, locally and in New York City.
*Regarding his assignment of photographing the mayor, police chief, and publisher: "I chose to photograph these three gentlemen because of their character. I wanted to bring that out in their portraits."*

**Cecil & Doris Trueblood** are a husband and wife photographic team. He is the technician; she is the artist. They are faculty members in the College of Education at Penn State.
*"We chose to photograph buildings and participated from a desire to communicate to people the rich mosaic of new and historic buildings that provide educational, cultural and social activities to those who visit and live in the State College area."*

**Denise Wagner** is a local artist with experience in photography, oils, acrylics, and computer graphics. She is currently a full-time graphic artist with Penn State and holds an associate degree in liberal arts.
*"I use my photographic skills to create images that reflect my concern for our diminishing wildlife and rural habitat. I feel that photography is an excellent medium to educate others to a greater awareness of the ecological treasures that are disappearing."*

**Bill Wallace** is a videographer and cinematographer for WPSX-TV, the public television station affiliated with Penn State.
*"I've always been attracted to the verité, off-the-cuff, grab-it-as-it-goes-by photographic style. I took this day as an impromptu, unplanned event. I drove around for a bit, as I used to do when I was shooting news for television, looking for whatever caught my eye."*

**Steve Welch** owns and operates The Mountainview Studios, a photography business in College Township. From 1990 through 1992, he operated a photography studio in the Borough.

Steve came to State College when he was three years old and attended State College schools as he grew up. He graduated from Penn State with a degree that combined photography and business administration. Steve's wife, Tina, is also a Penn State graduate.
*"I feel that I am a lucky man because I have been able to make a living at a craft that many consider a hobby. I wish the 'Day in the Life of State College' was one month and two days later, because the best thing that has ever happend to me happened in State College on October 14, 1995 … the birth of my son, Griffin."*

**Don Werb** is retired from the U.S. Government Civil Service. For several years he worked at the U.S. Government Aviation Research Center where he was a photographer producing high-speed scientific atomic-level images.
*"My lengthy State College relationship began when I married Margery Susan Youngel, the daughter of State College's first chief of police. We were married at Our Lady of Victory Church and had our reception at The Nittany Lion Inn. Over the following thirty-*

four years, we have visited State College annually. I wanted to participate in this project because we have such close ties here."

**Jennifer Wittaker** was a student at Penn State and was assigned to photograph State College for her graphic design class.
*"Since I grew up in State College, the people and places are so familiar to me that I tend to take them for granted. This assignment gave me an opportunity to take a closer look at the beauty of this town and to capture it for others to view."*

**Donna F. Williams** has taken photographs for ten years in her job as director of public relations for Centre Community Hospital.
*"The hospital is an important element in State College. I wanted the hospital to be a part of the Centennial celebration. I photographed in the Emergency Department because in nearly every hour of every day, someone comes in the door needing our immediate help."*

**Steve Williams** is a video producer-director for the College of Agricultural Sciences at Penn State. He is also a fine-arts photographer specializing in large format, black and white photography of natural and man-made landscapes. *"I consider photography an avenue for personal exploration. I find out more about myself from my photography. I've often called photography, 'a poor man's therapy.'"*

**Christine E. Wilson** participated in this project on assignment for her graphic design class at Penn State.
*"I prefer to photograph inanimate objects. I find that I can express myself emotionally through making portraits of them. I suppose this can be characterized as an editorial approach to photography because I infuse objects with meaning. I also have a fine-arts approach to my work, in that I enjoy tinting black and white photographs to make them appear other than they are in reality."*

**Kim Winck** works for the Center for Academic Computing at Penn State. She assists Penn State faculty members in creating multimedia courseware. She also works part-time fabricating jewelry for a local goldsmith.
*"I wanted to be part of this Centennial project because I grew up in this area, and I know it well. This was a perfect outlet for my creative interests."*

**Sean Zembower** was a kindergarten student at Lemont Elementary School on September 12, 1994. This academic year, he is a first grader at Panorama Village Elementary School.
*"I really liked my Lemont kindergarten teacher, Mrs. Domin. She was very nice. She showed me how to use the camera so that I could take pictures of my friends in kindergarten. At home, I have two pet cats. One is Hobbes and one is Maggie. I like to swim, to play the piano, and sing. I like to work on my computer."*

**The Corps of Centennial Photographers**
On Sunday afternoon, September 11, 1994, the day before the official shoot, the Corps of Centennial Photographers gathered in the Fraser Street Plaza to pick up their press passes and to be briefed about their assignments. In an address to the photographers, Arnold Addison, Chairman of the State College Centennial Commission, thanked them for their participation and reminded them of the historical significance of the images they were about to make the next day.
*Steve Williams*

## *Participating Photographers*

Nearly 200 photographers submitted more than 4500 images to this project. Only 234 of these images are in this book. Others will appear in newspaper and magazine articles, exhibits, slide shows, and other audio visual productions.

The State College Centennial Commission gratefully acknowledges the creative contribution of the following 197 photographers — for without them, this photo-documentation project would not exist.

The work of these photographers will be preserved in the Penn State Room of Pattee Library as part of the Pennsylvania State University Archives, where they will remain as a pictorial sample of life in State College in the mid-1990s.

| | | | |
|---|---|---|---|
| Blossom Aberg | Roger Cuffey | Drew C. Frank | Norma Keller |
| Linda Andrews | Maryann Curione | Lurene Frantz | P. Tyson Kendig |
| Ellen J. Aschenbrenner | Gary J. Daley | Rod Fye | Laurence King |
| Zhanna Aseyeva | Ronald A. Davis | Jennifer Garringer | Bridgette Kloecker |
| Lisa Badger | Sandy DeMarco | Matthew L. Garrity | Andrea Kohler |
| Mike Ballard | Marion R. Deppen | Julia Geis | Stefanie La Bella |
| Robert M. Baumbach | James R. DeTuerk | Jonathan Georgopulos | Sue P. LaBrecque |
| John Bellanti | Warren DeWitt | Robert Gevanthor | Erik Larson |
| Adam Bergeman | John Dickison | Donna Gibbons | Jock Lauterer |
| Arthur Beward | Kim Dionis | Danielle Goldberg | Jason Lefebure |
| David E. Beyerle | Richard H. Dixon | Clarissa I. González | Edward Leos |
| Stacie Bird | Linda Domin | Rick Habacivch | Marc B. Levey |
| Lindsay Bisel | Marian Cannon Dornell | Jennifer Hall | Karen Lintner |
| Arthur Boller | Abbie Eden | Mary Sue Henszey | Pat Little |
| Matthew F. Brashears | Scott Elmquist | LaToya Herd | Rebecca Logan |
| Roberta Burkhart | Kelly Enscore | Bryan Hicks | Bryon Lomas |
| Brendon Cable | Robert L. Fantauzzo | Brian Hill | Kathy D. Long |
| Susan Calhoun | Ralph Fearing | Farley M. Hill | Michele Marchetti |
| Curtis Chan | Kayla Fetzer | Jill Hoffman | Peter S. Marshall |
| Lois R. Chavern | Bobbi Fisher | Kaitlin Hoover | Helena Lukas Martemucci |
| Li Chen | Kim N. Fisher | Andrea Hurley | Tonya Lynn Martin |
| Alice E. Clark | Randy Fisher | Michael T. Jesky | Jay C. Mastalerz |
| James Collins | Charles A. Fitzgerald | Clarence D. Johnson, Jr. | Jared Matthews |
| Anne Quinn Corr | John C. Flohr | Ben Jones | Judith A. Maya |
| Alexander Cross | Scott Flohr | Denny Kaltreider | Anna Maria McDannel |
| Richard L. Crowley | Rita Foderaro | Barbara J. Kasales | Heather McDermott |

Stephen L. McGregor

Annette Shirey McHugh

Pamela A. McHugh

Jean McManis

Russell V. Meyers

I. Jeanne Miller

Kimberly Millone

James Molony

Chuck Mong

Erman M. Moon

Eugene W. Moon

Suzanne H. Motley

Trevor Muffley

Julie L. Nash

Donna M. Neufer

My Linh Nguyen

Akua Nti

Howard P. Nuernberger

Terran Ondik

Kristen Opdenhoff

Chris O'Reilly

Richard S. Orr

Raegan Owens

Linda J. Pagani

David S. Palermo

Mark Palmer

Philip I. Park

Devin M. Pedzwater

Elizabeth H. Pennock

Roger Pennock, Jr.

Robert Petkac

Renae Pickering

Mark Pliner

Michele Polignone

Todd Pope

Michael Poulin

Robert J. Price

Chad M. Rachild

H. A. Rader

Anne M. Raupach

Cristine Rebersdorf

Paul Resch

Sophie Richmond

Leigh Anne Riskosky

Nova Ritchey

Jeffrey R. Ritter

Paul D. Ruby

Jamie Rutkoski

Kankindi Rwego

Julz Salewski

Cathy Seith

Mark Selders

Deepa Sen

Stephanie Seraydarian

Jennifer Shapira

Ellen M. Sherwood

Alan John Sidwar

Michelle Singleton

Mark Smeal

Carolyn Clinefelter Smith

Eric Smith

Mary Lou Snitger

Jill Snyder

Lynne Sobel

Kristin Breslin Sommese

Lanny Sommese

Ann Marie Sradomski

Leif Steiner

Susie Stitzer

Judy Strayer

Allen Strickler

Shelby Thayer

Nathanial Thomas

Lois Todd

Steve Tressler

Cecil Trueblood

Doris Trueblood

Denise Wagner

Bill Wallace

Robin Ward

Jackie Watson

Steve Welch

Don Werb

Richard L. Westover

Jennifer Whittaker

Donna F. Williams

Steve Williams

Christine E. Wilson

Kim Winck

Deb Worthen

Landis Wright

Quentin Wright

Sean Zembower

## *Recognition*

### State College Centennial Commission
*Arnold Addison*, Chairman
*Lurene Frantz*, Executive Director

*John A. Brutzman*
*John D. Dittmar*
*Anita J. Genger*
*Pete Jeffries*
*Janet Knauer*
*Nadine Kofman*
*Robert Kucas*
*Lilly Nichol*
*Connie Randolph*
*Karen P. Shute*
*Carolyn Clinefelter Smith*
*Diane Sweetland*
*Henry L. Yeagley, Jr.*

### Borough of State College
*Bill Welch*, Mayor
*Peter S. Marshall*, Borough Manager
*Ronald A. Davis*, Assistant Borough Manager
*Ernest C. Dabiero*, Purchasing Officer
*Joy Farrow*, Administrative Secretary
*Michael S. Groff*, Finance Director
*Gladys Mechling*, Finance Department Secretary
*Norma J. Crater*, Accounting Supervisor
*Terree Knapik*, Accounting Secretary

### State College Borough Council
*Jean W. McManis*, President
*R. Thomas Berner*
*Thomas E. Daubert*
*Maryann Haas*
*Janet K. Knauer*
*Ruth K. Lavin*
*Felicia Lewis*
*Jerry R. Wettstone*

### Book Production
PROJECT DIRECTORS
*Maryann Curione*
*Lurene Frantz*
*Steve Williams*

BOOK DESIGNERS
*Gretl Collins*
*James Collins*

EDITORS-IN-CHIEF
*Maryann Curione*
*Lurene Frantz*

WRITER/RESEARCHER
*Maryann Curione*

COMPUTER CONSULTING &
SUPPORT
*Ken Rosenberry*

TEXT ADVISORS
*Ronald A. Davis*
*Sally Heffentreyer*
*Nadine Kofman*
*William M. Mahon, III*
*Jean W. McManis*
*Jacqueline Melander*
*Bill Welch*

PHOTO EDITORS
*Maryann Curione*
*Kim Dionis*
*Lurene Frantz*
*Jock Lauterer*
*Edward Leos*
*Marc B. Levy*
*I. Jeanne Miller*
*Paul Ruby*
*Cathy Seith*
*Jean Turgeon*
*Steve Welch*
*Steve Williams*

IMAGE CATALOGUING
*Jean Birnie*
*Marge Knapp*
*Ellie Lindstrom*
*Joan Storch*

CONCEPT DEVELOPERS
*Bonnie Marshall*
*Peter S. Marshall*
*William E. Marshall*

PHOTOGRAPHERS'
ASSIGNMENTS
*Doris Hufnagle*
*Tom King*
*Chris Strehlo*

COMMITTEE FOR
CENTENNIAL SPONSORS
*Richard Barrickman*
*Robert W. Groves, III*
*Robert W. Potter*

COMMITTEE FOR
CENTENNIAL
BENEFACTORS
*Joan Brower*
*Michael F. Desmond*
*Ann Guss*
*Marilynne Hollis*
*Pete Jeffries*
*Rich Kalin*
*Karen P. Shute*
*Diane Sweetland*

BOOK SIGNINGS
*Marian Cannon Dornell*
*Tom King*
*I. Jeanne Miller*

CENTENNIAL LOGO DESIGN
*Cheryl Weisz*

COMPUTER IMAGING OF
CENTENNIAL LOGO
*David McGaffin*

**Project Offices & Support**

DOWNTOWN STATE COLLEGE
*Robert J. Price*
Executive Director
*Sally Krout*
Executive Assistant

CENTRE REGION CODE ADMINISTRATION & HOUSING—FIRE INSPECTION OFFICE
*Harry J. Burd*
*David Felice*
*Paul Freeman*
*Scott Fry*
*Adam Scheidell*
*Robert Wagner*

STATE COLLEGE PUBLIC WORKS
Duane Wolfe

COLLEGE TOWNSHIP MUNICIPAL BUILDING
*C. Thomas Lechner*
Township Manager
*Beulah L. Houser*
Receptionist

COLLEGE TOWNSHIP COUNCIL MEMBERS
*Janet Sulzer*
Chairwoman
*Fred E. Smith*
Vice-Chairman
*Chris Exarchos*
*Max Hartswick*
*Lee Shields*

**Photographic Exhibits**
*Maryann Curione*, Curator

**Photographic Printing for the Book & Exhibits**
SHECKLER PHOTOGRAPHICS CUSTOM LAB
*Barbara Hughes*
*Jon Sheckler*
*Lew Sheckler*

**Exhibition Matting & Framing**
OLD MAIN FRAME SHOP & GALLERY
*Kathleen Davies*
*Evelyn deRezenze*
*Marie Librizzi*
*Janet McKenna*
*Anne Sullivan*

**Press Passes**
COLLEGE OF AGRICULTURAL SCIENCES, PENN STATE
*Steve Williams*
*Pete Kauffman*

**Exhibit Site Coordinators**
ARTS IN EDUCATION PROGRAM
*Jennene Lundy*

BROOKLINE VILLAGE
*Lori Pacchioli*

CENTRE COMMUNITY HOSPITAL
*Donna F. Williams*
*Wilda Stanfield*

THE DAILY GRIND: A COFFEEHOUSE
*Ed & Debbie Molin*

ENCORE BOOKS GALLERY
*Gretchen Hyle*
*Allison Shea*

THE FILM CENTER
*Robin Baker*
*Mark Selders*

HUB GALLERIES PENN STATE
*Ann Shields*

PATTEE LIBRARY PENN STATE
*Jennifer Olsen*

SCHLOW MEMORIAL LIBRARY
*Betsy Allen*
*Martha Musser*

STATE COLLEGE POST OFFICE
*Felix DeSantis*

**Exhibit Receptions**
*JoAnn Lew*, Coordinator
*Maru Cross*
*Jean Eggert*
*Wilna Kesler*
*Joyce Moon*
*Jane Sheeder*

**Slide Shows Producers**
*Stacie Bird*
*Howard Nuernberger*
*Steve Williams*

**Slide Shows Director & Sound Designer**
*H. A. Rader*

**Slide Shows Event Coordinators**
*Robert M. Baumbach*
*Denny Kaltreider*

**Slide Shows Site Coordinators**
PENN STATE
*Mary Johnston,*
*Karen Ann Rugh*

SCHLOW MEMORIAL LIBRARY
*Betsy Allen*
*Patricia Griffith*

Materials from this project will be preserved in the Penn State University Archives.
*Lee Stout*
University Archivist
*Jackie Esposito*
Assistant University Archivist
*The staff of the University Archives*

**Digital Image Archiving**
*Paul M. Fanelli*
Director, Business Development Higher Education Markets, Eastern Area Eastman Kodak Company
*Sally Kalin*
Coordinator, Computer Based Resources & Services, Pattee Library, Penn State

SPECIAL THANKS
Bi Lo Foods
CPI Photo Finish

## Contributors

Our thanks to the following for their generous contributions to the State College Centennial Celebration and for their specific support for this historical photo-documentation project.

### Sponsors

*Centre Daily Times*
*The Corner Room*
*Eastman Kodak Company*
*The Film Center*
*HRB Systems*
*Kissinger Bigatel & Brower Realtors*
*Mellon Bank*
*Old Main Frame Shop & Gallery*
*PNC Bank*
*Rittenhouse Family—McDonald's*
*Sheckler Photographics Custom Lab*
*Uni-Marts*

### Benefactors

*Arnold & Nancy Addison*
*Martha A. Adams*
*Associated Realty*
*Janet Atwood*
*Aurum Goldsmiths*
*Centre Community Hospital*
*Richard F. & and JoAnne M. DeFluri*
*The Michael F. Desmond Family*
*Patricia Farrell*
*Robert E. Fleck & Associates*
*John & Lurene Frantz*
*Sidney & Helen Friedman*
*Bruce & Susan Heim*
*James & Suzi Hess*
*Pete & Millie Jeffries*
*Rich & Sally Kalin*
*John & JoAnn Lew*
*John & Mary Madore*
*Edward L. Mattil*
*Northwest Savings Bank*
*Omega World Travel*
*Jim & Barbara Palmer*
*PennTerra Engineering*
*Robert W. Potter*
*Rider Auto*
*Paul & Dotty Rigby*
*Lance & Ellen Shaner*
*Robert E. & Karen P. Shute*
*Thomas L. & Carolyn C. Smith*
*Virginia Keeler Smith*
*John & Cindy Solic*
*Gerald Bernard Maxwell Stein*
*Edwin & Grace Antes Strong*
*Sweetland Engineering & Associates*
*Tinderbox Gifts*
*Tri-County Oral Facial Surgeons, P.C.*

*"Photography is a medium
that is instantly immediate to everybody.
If photography has a use that justifies itself,
it is the good that it can do
by having ordinary people show their community
back to themselves."*

---

EDWARD LEOS

CENTENNIAL PHOTOGRAPHER